T. S. ELIOT

The Pattern in the Carpet

T. S. ELIOT
The Pattern in the Carpet

ELISABETH SCHNEIDER

University of California Press
BERKELEY   LOS ANGELES   LONDON

University of California Press
Berkeley and Los Angeles, California
University of California Press, Ltd.
London, England
Copyright © 1975, by
The Regents of the University of California
ISBN: 0-520-02648-9
Library of Congress Catalog Card Number: 73-90655
Printed in the United States of America

Contents

Acknowledgments

Even a slight essay on the poetry of T.S. Eliot can scarcely be composed today without incurring more debts than one can well enumerate, or remember, or distinguish. Among those that will be self-evident in the pages that follow, debts to Eliot's own prose writings stand out most prominently. These and other obligations, so far as I can sort them out, are recorded in the text and notes, I trust without serious omission. But several studies of Eliot's work by previous writers should be singled out here for my continuing obligation to them: Donald Gallup's indispensable *T.S. Eliot: A Bibliography* (in the revised edition of 1969) first of all, for its precise chronology and its record of Eliot's uncollected prose writings; then F.O. Matthiessen's *The Achievement of T.S. Eliot*, to which all subsequent work on Eliot is directly or indirectly indebted; Grover Smith's *T.S. Eliot's Poetry and Plays*, especially valuable for its comprehensive record of sources and allusions; Hugh Kenner's *The Invisible Poet: T.S. Eliot*, valuable for its wide range and critical perspectives (even when the latter differ from one's own); the late Herbert Howarth's book, misleadingly modest in its title, *Notes on Some Figures behind*

T.S. Eliot; and, not least, Valerie Eliot's facsimile edition of the typescript and manuscript of *The Waste Land*, of which both the text and the editor's introduction and notes have been exceedingly useful. Much that is contained in the several writings of Dame Helen Gardner and Leonard Unger has been of value. Two excellent studies published in 1972, Bernard Bergonzi's short *T.S. Eliot* and John D. Margolis's *T.S. Eliot's Intellectual Development, 1922-1939*, reached me after my own chapters had been completed and their joints almost too ossified for change. Had I met these books earlier I might have found myself on occasion employing their formulations instead of my own.

Three friends and former colleagues, Professors Irwin Griggs, Marvin Mudrick, and Alan Stephens, and subsequently also Professor William Pritchard of Amherst College generously took time from busy lives to read my work in manuscript, to its advantage and to its author's reassurance that despite the crowded shelf a place may remain for yet another book on Eliot. Professor Hugh Kenner generously lent me a prepublication copy of his paper "The Urban Apocalypse," delivered before the English Institute in 1972.

I am indebted to Mrs. T. S. Eliot for permission to consult manuscript material in the Houghton Library at Cambridge and (before publication of *The Waste Land Facsimile*) that in the Berg Collection of the New York Public Library; also to Mrs. Lola L. Szladits, Curator of the Berg Collection and Mr. Rodney Dennis of Houghton for courtesy in making the material conveniently available.

The staff of the Library of the University of California at Santa Barbara have provided assistance of many kinds with unfailing patience and courtesy; though many have helped, I think particularly of the expertise of Mr. Martin Silver of the music division in his efforts to help me locate the sheet music of the "Shakespearian Rag." In this connection also I am grateful to Mr. Bill Lichtenwanger of the Library of Congress's Music Division, who with the sheet music in front of him sang part of that rag to me over the long distance telephone. The libraries of the University of California at Berkeley and Los Angeles have enabled me to examine certain of their materials conveniently, as has the Library of the University of Virginia. I am indebted, also, to the Regents of the University of California for a grant in aid of research and to my research assistant of several years ago, now Dr. John Reid of San Francisco.

Parts of several chapters, in a different version written in 1970, appeared as "Prufrock and After: The Theme of Change" in *PMLA* in 1972; small portions of the chapter on *Prufrock* had been written still earlier in simpler terms for notes in an anthology *Poems and Poetry* and in *The Range of Literature* (edited with Albert L. Walker and Herbert E. Childs). I am obliged to the Modern Language Association and D. Van Nostrand for the partial re-use of these.

Finally, I should like to thank Mr. William McClung and his associates at the University of California Press for kindness, patience, and intelligence shown as the manuscript has been making its way into print.

A Note on the Notes

Notes of reference are printed at the end of the volume, following the list of "Texts and References." Notes of substance (with abridged references as needed) are printed in the text. It has not been found practicable to make this distinction quite absolute, but the reader with no interest in the source of information or quotation may be assured of losing little or nothing by ignoring the backnotes.

1

Introduction

Double vision, of sorts, is the aim: to look back and forth from the single poem or picture to the artist's entire work, aware of both simultaneously; to be aware of the signature of the artist written all over each work, a signature different each time but never altogether different; and to perceive something of the continuity persisting beneath development and change. It is a process every interested reader attempts, whether he means to or not, as he rereads the work of an author's lifetime, and he is probably best rewarded if he does it deliberately. Ever since *Ash Wednesday* succeeded *The Waste Land* we have been reading the poems of T.S. Eliot with something of this double vision, striving to contemplate each poem simultaneously as part and as whole, without loss to either. Eliot, however, presented unusual obstacles to a nice balance in this process, partly because the very fact that *The Waste Land was* succeeded by *Ash Wednesday* encouraged in many of us rather a split than a double vision. There was an additional reason, too, for Eliot's own most celebrated and most influential critical statements once appeared to license only a single-valued concentration upon the sterilized, virtually anonymous single work, or alternatively upon that work viewed with reference to an equally anonymous entity called "tradition," itself only a traceable thread in the even more impersonal history of culture.

Few pronouncements of Eliot ever exerted quite so powerful an influence upon the critical world as did the doctrine requiring of a poet the "extinction of personality." The essay launching that doctrine, "Tradition and the Individual Talent," informed its readers that the true poet, *as* poet, "has, not a 'personality' to express, but a particular medium": that the artist's progress in fact requires "a continual self-sacrifice, a continual extinction of personality"; for poetry "is not the expression of personality, but an escape from personality." Responding to this "depersonalization," the critic and the appreciative reader must ignore the existence of the poet himself. And poet though he was, Eliot did not shrink from the conclusion: "It is in this depersonalization that art may be said to approach the condition of science." The statement was being launched as a new doctrine of some importance: in the essay itself it is referred to with deliberate capitalization as "this Impersonal theory of poetry."

Published in the fall of 1919 and within a few years widely accepted without modification—possibly also without a close look—the doctrine became central to the literary education of two or three generations of readers, who now carefully avoided saying "poet"; it was the isolated "poem" one read and its isolated "persona" that one listened to. This, with certain related views, is still widely looked upon as Eliot's true critical position.

Yet within a few years of that original pronouncement, he himself without its being much noticed had begun to express surprise at the stir he had created and had begun to modify—for some purposes even reverse—his doctrine of depersonalization. "What every poet starts from," he now said, speaking of Shakespeare and Dante, "is his own emotions." Both Shakespeare and Dante were concerned with the "struggle—which alone constitutes life for a poet— to transmute his personal and private agonies into something rich and strange, something universal and impersonal." This was a correction of emphasis, not a rightaboutface; impersonality remained a criterion and presumably no reader need know what agonies of the poet lay behind the poem. In another two years, however, by 1929, Eliot had become convinced that the poet's own personality and private experience may show through the transparency of the verbal surface: Dante's *Vita Nuova*, he asserted, had obviously been "written around a personal experience," and he proceeded to speculate upon that experience. The verbal surface, then, might be recognizably marked by its biographical origin as well as derived from it, and this Eliot did not now consider a flaw, nor did he regard as improper a critical interest in the "facts," the biographical origins. In later comments he went much further, asserting that the reader hears and should hear the personal voice of the poet, who, for example in the dramatic monologue, normally "has put on the costume and make-up either of some historical character, or of one out of fiction": it is surely "the voice of the poet talking to other people, that is dominant." As such a statement can be made only with considerable straining about Browning, who was his ostensible example in this passage, we may take it as one of the many indirect clues to Eliot's own poems planted with deliberation through his prose. It also amounts nearly to a full retraction of his doctrine of 1919.

An earlier and equally significant departure from that original position, turning in a slightly different direction, had involved insistence that the reader see the whole of a poet's work as being itself a single work of art unified by a personality: "by 'work of art,'" he had observed, he there meant "the work of one artist as a whole." The fullest statement of this idea occurs in a passage on Shakespeare

dating from 1932, in which he appeared to place a higher
value upon the pattern of development from play to play
than upon even the best of the individual plays. Both the
theme and the technique of each play, Eliot said, appear
to have been "determined increasingly by Shakespeare's
state of feeling, by the particular stage of his emotional
maturity at the time." To see "the whole man," therefore,
we must perceive "the whole pattern formed by the sequence of plays." The degree to which a poet approaches
this unity of pattern through the variety of works that
make up his oeuvre, Eliot considered "one of the measures
of major poetry and drama." "The whole of Shakespeare's
work is *one* poem," he concluded, "united by one significant,
consistent, and developing personality"; and "it is the
poetry of it in this sense . . . that matters most."

After such modifications as these, the residual value
implicit in the original doctrine of depersonalization would
seem to be no more than a requirement of aesthetic
distancing, though Eliot never used that term for it. Even
in the days of his "impersonal theory," wishing that what
he considered the artistic failure of *Hamlet* might be more
fully understood, he expressed the wish that we might know
"under compulsion of what experience [Shakespeare] attempted to express the inexpressibly horrible" in that play.
In order to know this we should need "a great many facts"
in Shakespeare's biography, he said; though even if we had
them, the inmost truth would more than likely elude us,
might indeed be unknowable, something Shakespeare himself did not fully understand.[1]

These changing critical doctrines of Eliot closely reflect
his own poetic development. In spite of his rarely quite
genuine "impersonality" and his always quite genuine
reserve, he has in the end through his prose told us more
about his poetry than any other English poet I can think
of except perhaps Wordsworth: his best criticism, he himself said, was the by-product of his "private poetry-work-

shop; or a prolongation of the thinking" that had produced the poetry.[2] In spite of his reserve, too, we already know a few more "facts" about Eliot than we shall ever know of Shakespeare; and the interplay among external facts, critical writing, and poetry sheds frequent light upon what is in the end the object of primary interest, the poetry itself. In citing all these key statements of Eliot, I am allowing him to set the terms for a reading of his poems, in part. But only in part: readers, even critics, have their rights; and we do not read *Lear* only for the sake of what it tells us of its share in the "personality" of Shakespeare. We do, then, require that double vision of which I spoke at the outset.

Considered together, all the same, the writings of Eliot give evidence of a deliberate intention to unify the whole body of his poetry and plays quite as he saw Shakespeare's and Dante's work unified and marked by a single "developing personality." Pure biographical interpretation in the old sense (or, for that matter, in the Stracheyan or debased post-Stracheyan sense) is not what we need contemplate. Of course—with Dr. Johnson standing behind us—we should like to know all there is to know about Eliot the man: "there is nothing so minute or inconsiderable, that one would not rather know it than not," as Johnson declared, even to the knowledge of how to "hem a ruffle." And so, rather more than ruffles, of any writer whose work interests us. Yet in glancing back and forth between the work and the man we again hear the warning of Dr. Johnson, on learning that in youth he had been looked upon as a happy undergraduate: "Ah, Sir, I was mad and violent. It was bitterness which they mistook for frolick." Passages in Eliot's poems have been read interchangeably as bitterness and frolic. Reading them again at this distance of time, with whatever tact and caution we may be blessed with, we have still to mind the distinction, not an easy one, which rests upon identities and differences both

fundamental and subtle, between the "developing personality" traceable in a man's life (provided materials are at
hand) and that which is revealed or created in his work,
and between the work as a whole and the individual poem.
They are never quite the same nor ever quite different;
and they are indissoluble. Eliot knew, and in effect said,
this. His avenging ghost may hereafter be roused by
ineptness in the exercise of our double vision, but his
mature critical writing has licensed its composite principle—supposing this to require other licensing than its
natural roots in the complexities of life and art.

2

The Search for a Style

Punctilious of tie and suit
(Somewhat impatient of delay)
On the doorstep of the Absolute.
Spleen (from *Poems Written in Early Youth*)

The earliest development of Eliot as a poet is only broadly traceable. Dates and chronology of early poems remain uncertain, and a greater difficulty arises from there being few pieces out of which to construct a history. Whether because he wrote little or because much has been lost, scarcely more than a dozen poems now known are thought to have been written earlier than the dozen that appeared in *Prufrock and Other Observations* (1917); and of this small earlier handful two can only be dismissed as appallingly correct public graduation poems, speaking for schoolmates sailing forth across the harbor bar from Smith Academy or fair Harvard. Yet *Prufrock* (the poem, not the volume), apparently written mainly between 1909 and 1911 while Eliot was still in his early twenties, is not exactly a practice piece.

7

At school and as an undergraduate at Harvard Eliot
had appeared before his small public in the approved way,
not as a young writer with anything to say but as one
with a manner, or several manners; and by the date of
the smaller poems in the *Prufrock* volume, the manners
must have appeared as the elegantly bad ones of a cool,
cynical, bright, irreverent, and arrogant young man. Eliot
ended as elder statesman, upholding with conviction and
eloquence the cause of established religion, the course of
his journey having led from, among other things, a view
of the Church as Hippopotamus "wrapt in the old miasmal
mist" to a Christian faith that "all shall be well, and/
All manner of thing shall be well."

It is an interesting progress, though one not unique in
this century, for we remember the young sceptical Aldous
Huxley in the years when he knew the mystic as one who
"objectifies a rich feeling in the pit of the stomach into
a cosmology," and the tortuous course which the "rich
feeling," if that is what it was, eventually led him. There
are Evelyn Waugh also, and others, twentieth-century
analogues all, in their way, of the once young Romantic
radicals and sceptics Southey, Wordsworth, and Coleridge
more than a century earlier. Maturing of experience into
wisdom, or exhaustion of courage and energy into confor-
mity: the observer is tempted to judge according to his
own faith or temperament while his critical judgment lags.
And so to one critic Eliot's significant poetry ends with
The Hollow Men, while for another, everything before *Four
Quartets* is essentially preparatory and even the first
Quartet is in the main a corridor opening upon the last
retreat for worship, *Little Gidding*. Either picture of Eliot,
either judgment of his poetry, is caricature; and now that
we have the body of his work in at least a preliminary
perspective, we may try for a cooler view of that metamor-
phosis, over the years, in both matter and manner. What
makes the progression more than commonly interesting

is the fact that, as poet, Eliot both expressed and observed the whole.

Starting out as a youthfully accomplished conventional technician (with a noticeable preference for complex over easy rhyming), Eliot spoke at first in other men's voices, with results, despite an evident flair for language, somewhat but not spectacularly beyond those of the clever undergraduate. At sixteen the voice was Don Juan's, exercised with some of Byron's relish, in a tale of greedy monks; or it was the seventeenth-century lyricist's voice in extremely neat *carpe diem* verses, shading, after an interval at Harvard, into the *fin de siècle*'s withered flowers with "fragrance of decay." By 1908, at twenty, Eliot had grown enterprising enough to graft the grittier manner of John Davidson upon Swinburne's Proserpina:

Around her fountain which flows
With the voice of men in pain,
Are flowers that no man knows.
Their petals are fanged and red

. . . .

They sprang from the limbs of the dead.

Roses, however, along with vaguer flowers with or without fangs, soon gave way to satire, generally with fangs.

Though nearly all these verses were such as might be expected, in the first decade of the century, of a young man with considerable talent for smooth conventional versification and up-to-the-minute taste, one or two features of the work might have been noticed even then. For one thing, the young man was in no hurry to talk about himself. This was in part a natural outcome of his use of other men's voices: he was busy practicing his art and trying on attitudes by imitation. But one is aware also of a certain cautious unwillingness to give away any private world; no adolescent longings are allowed to creep in. A general reaction against Romanticism and its later faded

representatives was already under way, particularly at
Harvard among the young who listened, as Eliot did, to
Irving Babbitt. And it must be admitted that some of the
now forgotten poets of that day bared their souls with
an absence of dignity that must have intensified the
reserved Eliot's theoretical disapproval into a personal
dislike so acute that then, and for many years to come,
it blinded him even to poetic distinction if its tone were
less disengaged than his own; blinded him for years even
to the distinction of Yeats. Eliot's early verses, at any rate,
including the shorter poems of the *Prufrock* volume, are
nearly all as impersonal and unromantic as if their author
had already adopted his as yet unformulated principle of
"depersonalization."

SYMBOLISTS AND THEIR
ENGLISH CONTEMPORARIES

The discovery of his own voice came about mainly
through his encounter with Arthur Symons's *The Symbolist Movement in Literature* and the introduction through
this book to the French Symbolist poets themselves, particularly Jules Laforgue. "A very young man, who is himself
stirred to write, is not primarily critical or even widely
appreciative," Eliot wrote in a late essay that was half
an apology for his earlier failure to value Yeats. "He is
looking for masters who will elicit his consciousness of what
he wants to say himself, of the kind of poetry that is in
him to write. . . . The kind of poetry that I needed, to teach
me the use of my own voice, did not exist in English at
all; it was only to be found in French."[1]

Several English poets, however, writing at the turn of
the century, had provided more than a mere foretaste of
what the Symbolists were to offer Eliot. He had been
reading the English poets of the nineties, he tells us in
a late retrospect, "the only poets . . . who at that period
of history seemed to have anything to offer me as a

beginner." Several of these were writers who had escaped
the post-Romantic morass in which themes of nature and
love had become sodden, by turning for freshness and
"truth" to the urban and the everyday. There was W. E.
Henley—not the Henley of *Invictus* but the Henley of the
"In Hospital" and "London" sequences. *In Hospital* describes the patient anaesthetized on the operating table,
and in Number 23 of the sequence Eliot would have met
the street organ, the "magic lantern," April in the city,
"sprinkled pavements," details that we recognize again in
Prufrock and *Portrait of a Lady*. When in late years he
wrote a preface for a selection of poems by John Davidson,
Eliot took occasion to acknowledge early debts, particularly to "the author of *The City of Dreadful Night*" and
to Davidson, poet of London in the *Fleet Street Eclogues*,
The Thames Embankment, and *In the Isle of Dogs*. In
a late broadcast Eliot named among poets of the nineties
whom he had read with profit during his last days at school
or his first year or two at Harvard, Symons, Dowson ("one
or two poems" especially), and Davidson, of whom he still
admired other poems "very much indeed. . . . But it is
'Thirty Bob a Week' which made a terrific impact upon
me. And," he went on, "I think it [Davidson's poetry]
prepared me for initiation into the work of some of the
French symbolists, such as Laforgue, whom I came across
shortly after. But 'Thirty Bob a Week' has a very important
place in the development of my own poetic technique."
From Davidson and several of these other poets, he explained, he "got the idea that one could write poetry in
an English such as one would speak oneself. A colloquial
idiom. There was a spoken rhythm in some of their poems."[2]
Besides colloquial idiom, Eliot would have found in poems
of Davidson the city fog, the unromantic city moon, the
London Underground, dockyard, pier, barrel-organ, all
novel in English poetry; and with them came what to
Davidson were the "millions of useless souls" that shortly

began to people Eliot's own poems. Late in life Eliot ascribed partly to Baudelaire his discovery of the sordid city as a theme for poetry, but in certain poetry of the nineties, particularly in that of Davidson and James Thomson, the discovery had begun.

The Symbolists nevertheless did open doors for him that none of the "Nineties" poets writing in English could have opened, for in addition to their superiority as poets they came to him with the accidental but engaging glamour conferred by an only half-familiar language—a return gift to the English of the glamour that must earlier have helped glorify Poe in France. Eliot has said he was "passionately fond of" some French poetry long before he could translate it properly and confessed that he had never in fact been truly bilingual.[3] After his year at the Sorbonne (October 1910-July 1911) he became sufficiently accomplished to write verse himself in French, with assistance, but to the young man of 1909 French poetry—especially such poetry as that of the Symbolists—for linguistic reasons alone would have been exotic even while it projected the familiar sordid commonplaces of city life.

If only for this reason it would be Baudelaire in preference to Davidson who would be felt to underlie the "Unreal City" of *The Waste Land*, as Eliot implied in his notes to the poem, quoting "Fourmillante cité, cité pleine de rêves,/ Où le spectre en plein jour raccroche le passant." For it would be a fine and a new thing if he could create in his own language something approximating to the blend of the familiar and the strange which Baudelaire offers to an English reader not fully bilingual. In the *Prufrock* volume, Eliot seems occasionally to be straining for this by the doubtful means of direct linguistic imitation, when he replaces the "English one would speak oneself" by a not quite native and certainly not conversational idiom: "Regard that woman," he writes in the *Rhapsody on a Windy Night* and "remark the cat" and "regard the moon."

And the exclamation in *Prufrock*, "But how his arms and legs are thin!" is French, not English.

Except for this blend of the strange with the familiar, suggested by the French poets as he read them, and except for the much more important discovery of a congenial persona in Laforgue, Henley and Davidson along with James Thomson offered Eliot nearly all he needed. However, the prime discovery made through Symons' book was Laforgue, in whom Eliot encountered the "temperament akin to one's own" of which he spoke often in later years; and with recognition of the temperament came the "discovery of one's own form" and of the "poetic possibilities of [his] own idiom of speech," he said.[4] The dandyism, the irony mocking society and mocking himself, the ostentatiously formal-informal colloquialism of diction and inflection were all there and soon began to show in his own verse, for the mask that Laforgue had devised fitted Eliot nearly enough to point the way to his own, within which, after practising two close imitations of poems quoted by Symons, he found his first poetic freedom.[a]

The line between influence of the Symbolists and influence of the later Imagists is a sometimes blurred one, for both schools were concerned with the poetic handling of imagery. The value of the concrete to poetry had never been in question, and no problems had ever arisen—no theoretical problems at least—when imagery functioned within a narrative or discursive framework. Pure descrip-

[a] See the account in Howarth, *Notes*, pp. 103-109, and for recent fine discrimination between Symbolist and Imagist image, see Robert M. Adams in Litz, *Eliot*, pp. 139-142, 145. I am convinced, however, that the *persona* influencing Eliot was at least as much Laforgue-through-Symons as it was Laforgue direct; most of the clearly Laforguian side of Eliot is in fact right there in Symons—as well as some non-Laforguian bits. The line in *Prufrock*, "To have squeezed the universe into a ball," is probably not Marvell-direct but Marvell-by-way-of Symons, who wrote, "In Laforgue, sentiment is squeezed out of the world before one begins to play at ball with it."

tive writing as an extended form, however, has had an only half-prosperous history, and reaction against extended descriptive passages, even against poetry that expresses "powerful emotions" through set pieces of natural description, had been incipient even in the Romantic era where it so flourished. The discourse of Lessing on the limits of poetry and painting in the *Laokoon* had even then brought into question the effectiveness of descriptive writing, on the ground that movement, drama, change provide the natural continuity and are the dynamic power inherent in arts whose extension is temporal rather than spatial, a truth that had been recognized without benefit of theory, Lessing pointed out, from the time of Homer's "description" of the shield of Achilles. A narrative thread was therefore often deliberately employed in the nature poetry even of the Romantic poets, the rough outlines of Lessing's thesis being so striking and so easily communicable that a nineteenth-century writer had no need to have read the *Laokoon* itself in order to come under its influence.

This feature of the best descriptive poetry is a truism of elementary rhetorical studies, but it became also a link in modern literary history. For another means than narrative was sought, by both Symbolist and Imagist poets, of breaking down the static set piece of description without having to abandon to the painter and photographer most of the visual world, or to retain it only in ancillary capacities as metaphor, epithet, "background," or the brief phrase that vivifies narrative. The key was discontinuity. Imagery could be freed from explicit continuity and left to stand alone in brief juxtapositions that might have something of the force of metaphor without being actually referable to an abstraction. The classic examples of this kind of imagist poem are by Sandburg (not officially part of the club) in *Fog* and Pound in *In a Station of the Metro*:

The apparition of these faces in the crowd;
Petals on a wet, black bough.

Here is discontinuity in brevity of the whole and the normal discontinuity of all metaphor, accentuated by the separate concreteness of both of the juxtaposed elements, and in the Pound lines by the ostensibly noncommittal equality of the two images, which leaves conceptual interpretation of the equation entirely to the reader if he requires it. This, however, is a limited poetic genre, interest in which is apt to be quickly exhausted, though the haiku and variants of it attained a fairly lasting popularity.

In more extended forms, older poetry had occasionally developed by means of discontinuous imagery; there is no novelty in its doing so when the theme is explicit, as it is, for example, in the prolonged sequence of high-born maiden and rose embowered in Shelley. Sequences of images, however, when they are not bound together by an explicit theme and not so obviously related to each other that the theme is as good as explicit, were new. The problem reduces itself essentially to the ancient one of what to do with the visual world in a succession of words.

The discontinuities of *The Waste Land* and of many passages in Symbolist and Imagist poetry have complex origins, but they are rooted partly in this history of descriptive writing and its admitted problems. The eighteenth-century development of associationist psychology might have been expected to (but did not in fact) liberate the poetic image from narrative, descriptive, or logical continuity as poets who read Hartley became increasingly aware of the rationally inconsequent shifts and turns in the flow of our mental imagery and memory. Coleridge discussed the nature of association more than once in notebooks and letters, yet even he, who undoubtedly lived much with discontinuous trains of thought, did not introduce them into his poetry (even *Kubla Khan* is not quite an exception); and I find it hard to point to clear instances in English earlier than this century's stream-of-consciousness writing. The detached image appears occasionally in Romantic drama, but there the dramatist had

clearly taken his cue from Shakespeare, not Hartley; the
dramatic and psychological force of discontinuity was
something the Elizabethan and Jacobean dramatists knew
how to employ at crucial moments in tragedy, and Shakespeare knew further how both to heighten and transcend
the discontinuity in the supreme imaginative poetry of such
passages as Cleopatra's lines on the death of Antony:

> O, wither'd is the garland of the war,
> The soldier's pole is fall'n! Young boys and girls
> Are level now with men; the odds is gone,
> And there is nothing left remarkable
> Beneath the visiting moon.

Or the more obviously "realistic" discontinuities after
Hamlet has seen his father's ghost.

Similar discontinuities, or tangential continuity, once
confined to drama, appeared in the lyric with the advent
of the Symbolists, and today the nondramatic poem composed of fragmented imagery united, often loosely or idio-
syncratically, by a mood is commonplace, though it still
troubles some readers. Obviously, it is a form more open
than most to a variety of interpretation or response.
What does one make, for example, of the opening line of
Laforgue's *L'Hiver qui vient*—"Blocus sentimental! Messa-
geries du Levant!"—in the hands of two competent translators, rendered alternatively as "Sentimental Blockade!
Express from the rising sun!" and "Blockade of the senses!
Mail steamers from the Levant"? Does the context really
point to either, or to something else that both translators
have missed or that both have achieved despite their
differences? Similar questions lie at the heart of many
interpretive problems today within our own language.

THE "OTHER OBSERVATIONS"

The important poems in Eliot's first volume, *Prufrock
and Other Observations*, the *Rhapsody on a Windy Night*,

Portrait of a Lady, and *Prufrock*, are already sophisticated examples of this new direction, though they all retain, in a reduced role, a thread of narrative (and, in the case of *Prufrock*, also discursive) continuity.

The *Rhapsody on a Windy Night* represents the mood and thoughts of a dry brain in a dry season, strung upon the continuity of a solitary walk through city streets from street lamp to street lamp and from hour to hour in the hours past midnight. The outline is from another poet's moonlit walk in the early pages of *The City of Dreadful Night*: in that walk too, distance is marked by the succession of "street-lamps," which in turn "always burn" and "burn amidst the baleful glooms" and "burn along the silent streets," while time is marked as "the pitiless hours [which] like years and ages creep;" and Thomson's city presently turns into desert, "As I came through the desert thus it was." Eliot's midnight eye is more selective and economical, nominally more objective, and his results a good deal less murky. While Thomson fills his night with endless symbolic phantasmagoria and explicit outpourings of despair, Eliot writes a symbolist poem in which even the subjective opening stanza eschews direct expression of emotion.

> Twelve o'clock.
> Along the reaches of the street
> Held in a lunar synthesis,
> Whispering lunar incantations
> Dissolve the floors of memory
> And all its clear relations,
> Its divisions and precisions.
> Every street lamp that I pass
> Beats like a fatalistic drum, . . .

Objects seen and objects remembered slide into each other: the walker sees a whore and remembers unrelated trivia, sees a cat and remembers a young child and an old crab. Presiding over the night, the moon, ancient mistress of madness and imagination, dissolves the "floors" of rational, ordered memory, subjectivizing in her "lunar synthesis" objects seen and objects floating up from memories shaken free of rational order by the lunar dissociation, "as a madman shakes a dead geranium." [b] It is a city moon, a moon disfigured, that is beheld by the walker; and the key to her synthesis of his mood lies in images of the crooked and the twisted, both literal and symbolic: crooked eye, crooked pin, crooked tear in the woman's dress, twisted branch and broken rusty spring; automatic meaningless graspings after what is worthless, offspring of the twisted: cat reaching for butter that is rancid, child for a toy not his or scarcely desired, voyeur reaching for others' lives, crab for a dry stick. Twisted images of present and past have drifted together, and soon the moon and the whore too drift together; they are one, and she is mad. As whore she had reached out automatically for a customer, but she is alone. From these phantasmal floating images of the distorted and the worthless is crystallized a sense of deep disgust, which had been present all the while, the self-disgust which from the beginning had summoned and synthesized the "crowd of twisted things" and their stale smells: this is the self one had walked out with and the self one comes home to, "the last twist of the knife."

In its form, though it follows a narrative sequence, the *Rhapsody* is essentially created by its thematic pattern of imagery linked by similarities plain enough to be unambiguous yet imaginative enough to do the work wanted, establishing the mood: there is nothing indeterminate here as there is in *L'Hiver qui vient.* The hard-edged mechanical sequence of hour after hour, street lamp after lamp has the double value of keeping the floating imagery within formal, contrasting bounds at the same time as it under-

[b] For this dazzling image, cf. the opening of Laforgue's *Derniers Vers X*: "O géraniums diaphanes, guerroyeurs sortilèges,/ Sacrilèges monomanes!" Eliot made a point of quoting these lines later in his essay on "The Metaphysical Poets" (1921).

lines the hopeless continuum of disgust. Young as he is, the poet is now expert; dissolving the rational floors of mind and memory, he still holds a tight rein on the phantasmagoria that results.

Portrait of a Lady, which appears to have been written before either *Prufrock* or the *Rhapsody*, is inferior to both, but contains memorable passages and is of interest as prefiguring a later technique. Its carefully indicated continuities of time and place are conventional: three scenes marked by seasons, tea-time in December, April, and October, through which the lady is portrayed vividly but as a "type" figure and not subtly: she is the middle-aged woman clutching desperately at the young man, making claims upon him through flattery and assumed intimacy, with indirect but gross appeals to pity. The tone and idiom of such a woman are neatly, maliciously caught. We know how she speaks and what her grasping does to him from her first words, "I have saved this afternoon for you." How does one meet this when one has not asked to have it saved?

Notably the best things in the poem are delineations not of the woman but of her effect upon the young man, the "I" of the poem. Her self-pity thinly disguised as brave resignation, "I shall sit here, serving tea to friends," wrings from him the unspoken "How can I make a cowardly amends/ For what she has said to me?" This must be the classic formulation of that complex mental state in which one feels irrationally guilty for the other's breach, not one's own, or guilty for one's inability to respond to a demand that should never have been made. At his final visit her refrain, "serving tea to friends," elicits from him the again unspoken images

> And I must borrow every changing shape
> To find expression . . . dance, dance
> Like a dancing bear,
> Cry like a parrot, chatter like an ape.

Dancing bear, talking parrot, chattering ape—the discomfort of being called upon to be human when one is not quite human. These are the durable moments in the poem, and such moments represent the early Eliot's best perceptions of feeling, a half-agonized, guilt-tinged embarrassment.

In each scene of the *Portrait* Eliot employs, but without the absolute success of its use in *Prufrock*, the device of a striking discontinuity of imagery to express abrupt revulsion of feeling: "Let us take the air, in a tobacco trance."— Let him escape from this oppressively personal talk, these embarrassing claims; let him admire the bad sculpture of public monuments, be the kind of man who checks his watch by every clock, who reads comics and the sporting page; let him be the man in the street. The speaker is not such a man; he is saying only, with intensity, "Let me get out of here!" Throughout, the poem has to do with characters, subjective attitudes, and feelings; and throughout, Eliot's presentation is by imagery, often discontinuous and never interpreted by any usual means of reference. Its main departure from Browning's dramatic monologues, from which it so obviously descends, lies in these discontinuities and, on the other hand, in Eliot's efforts to unify the poem by the imposition of recurrent musical images that range from Paderewski playing Chopin to cracked cornets, broken violins, street pianos—a pattern, however, that in this poem seems arbitrarily imposed: we see the young poet thinking up the device.

Hitherto Eliot had been occupied mainly with establishing a style, a tone, a language. But for themes was he to confine himself forever to ironic observations of Aunt Helen Slingsby's butler? The moody midnight walk of the *Rhapsody* reaches a different level; so does the *Portrait* at moments; and the much admired *La Figlia che Piange* may be thought to do so in some respects: many readers have felt in this poem a welcome warmth and a welcome absence of acid, though it is hard to see how this impression can survive more than casual readings. There is a lovers' parting; the girl is weeping, with flowers in her arms and sunlight in her hair. The lover is both the poet and not the poet; he would leave her both "as the soul leaves the body torn and bruised," and also in "some way" that is "simple and faithless as a smile and shake of the hand." The Laforguian irony is apparent even without the line of Laforgue which it closely approximates (Simple et sans foi comme un bonjour).[5] But the irony does not cast its light beyond its particular line, and I find no tone, not even a paradoxical one, and no imaginative reality that might hold the poem together. It reads as if the author had wished to turn himself free for a romantic moment in a romantic world without paying the price of admission or commitment; the romantic and the ironic elements are not adjusted to each other, and the whole poem comes out not as something subtle but as something slightly amorphous—an interesting failure, but a failure all the same, the statue, never seen, turned human in vain.

From the beginning, Eliot had known how not to give himself away embarrassingly in his poetry, but he had scarcely learned how to do this without being trivial. Nearly all but the three main poems completed by 1917, as well as some of those published in the 1920 volume, are little more than clever but superficial jeux d'esprit. *Mr. Apollinax*, to be sure, when one knows that its subject is Bertrand Russell, is funny at a depth of funniness (perhaps double-edged) that lifts it out of the class of the Cousin Nancys and Aunt Helens. The indisputable master-piece among the early poems, however, is *The Love Song of J. Alfred Prufrock.*

3

Prufrock

O sad Fraternity, do I unfold
    Your dolorous mysteries shrouded from of yore?
Nay, be assured; no secret can be told
    To any who divined it not before:
None uninitiate by many a presage
Will comprehend the language of the message, . . .

The City of Dreadful Night
from the Proem

Granted the limited excellence of the *Rhapsody* and the brilliance of a few passages in the *Portrait of a Lady, The Love Song of J. Alfred Prufrock* remains the one major poem of Eliot's earlier years (Leavis's preference for the *Portrait* duly noted). Of all that were written before he was twenty-five, it is the most serious; it is also the most personal and except for the *Rhapsody*, which is essentially all mood, and for certain Laforgue-through-Sweeney elements in the *Preludes*, it is the most subjective. But it stands alone also on another count, for in it Eliot approached for the first time a theme that would engage him, under a variety of aspects, through most of his major poems and plays, the theme of subjective change.

The most widely talked of event in Eliot's life was his conversion from scepticism to religious belief. Though unattended by anything spectacular on the poet's part— there were no public displays of confession and the convert became merely an Anglo-Catholic layman, not a priest or monk, or candidate for sainthood—his conversion was nevertheless rather a spectacular event in the intellectual and literary world, and criticism has been busy with it ever since. That change as the public knew it, however, is not quite in itself his poetic theme. What we see, looking at his work in perspective, is his long preoccupation, appearing most markedly in the poetry, with the process itself of subjective change: his concern, that is, not only with the end or cause, with what one may change from or to, but with the feeling of change itself: how possible it is, how easy or how hard; what the experience may be like of attempting to transform wish into will, will into belief and then dedication.

Thinking of these questions, one realizes that the subject has not often been explored by other poets. Among the Victorian "poets of doubt" we do not find quite this; and one has only to think of Donne or Hopkins to realize how special the theme is in Eliot. "Batter my heart," Donne will say; and Hopkins, "Thou heardst me truer than tongue confess/ Thy terror." But when Eliot says, "I rejoice, having to construct something upon which to rejoice," though the mode of paradox may remind one of Donne, the meaning does not. Here God does not, either, as with Hopkins, seize possession of man's self and will; in Eliot the "rejoicing," such as it is, is willed within the human self. Change as process, I am inclined to believe, may have engaged Eliot at a deeper level even than did its content or result—deeper, that is, than the actual Christian view of life arrived at, in saying which I do not in the least

belittle the importance or reality of his Christian commitment. The problem of change, at any rate, is consciously
and intimately followed through a succession of major
poems beginning, unpromisingly it might be thought, with
Prufrock, where the question is first posed.

The *Love Song of J. Alfred Prufrock* is many things,
and it should not be distorted merely to prove a point.
Yet at its most abstract level it does ask a central question,
"Is inner change possible?" and answers No, not anyhow
for Prufrock or his kind. Within the poem, the answer is
final though ultimately it was not so for Eliot. In dramatic
terms Prufrock's question is of course not nearly so broad,
and his individual case is too sharply presented to be felt
as the mere shell for a nut of abstraction. The poem is
therefore not primarily a symbolic representation of this
or any theme; on the contrary, it reads as though it has
sprung directly from a wish to set down as precisely as
possible what it feels like to be Prufrock; but as this does
not feel comfortable, the question of possible change is
inherent in the subject. Very likely such a theme was not
part of Eliot's first conscious intention, for he had evidently
set out to do a portrait modeled upon the pattern of
Browning's dramatic monologues, with time, place, and
revealing situation conscientiously set forth through the
character's speech, the whole to be modernized by means
of urban imagery, by adaptations of Symbolist technique,
and by the conception of a character that is a conscious
hybrid of the poet's self and Laforgue, made subtle through
the poet's own self-awareness. Yet the question of possible
change is unmistakably central to the final poem; if it
crept in through underground channels, that circumstance
makes it no less significant.

In the poem Prufrock speaks at a moment of decision.
"Let us go and make out visit," he says, and the Browning-
esque immediacy of time and place, given at once a new
dimension by the foreshadowing image of the sky "like

a patient etherised," leads to the central question: Shall he or dare he propose to a woman? The answer being no, the title is ironic: he will never sing his love song, nor will the mermaids ever sing to him. The rise and fall of the merest possibility of action, dramatized through imagery and the changing moods and tenses of verbs, provides a structure for the soliloquy from the initial "let us go," through the hesitations: "there will be time . . . time to turn back. . . . Do I dare disturb the universe? . . . And how should I begin? *Shall* I say. . .?" With the shift in these last words to a future indicative verb a little more than halfway through the poem, Prufrock having now brought himself to contemplate action not as reverie but as actual possibility, the question of *whether* advances for a moment to the question of *how*: "Shall" he say he does not wish to spend a lonely life looking on at others' lives from a window ledge, an empty room behind him? His vacillations of will have moved cautiously toward a possible if still somewhat meager affirmation, the subjunctive *should I* giving way momentarily to the more vivid future, *shall I*. But the will's approach to action generates its own automatic reversal and flight, conveyed through the grotesque central image of the poem, which embodies Prufrock's recognition of what essentially he is:

> I should have been a pair of ragged claws
> Scuttling across the floors of silent seas—

a subhuman crustacean, doubly dehumanized by the synecdoche of claws even beyond its identity as crab or lobster, and moving, a cold solitary being, in armored solitude on the sea floor. [a]

---

[a] I do not believe the image represents, as some writers have maintained, the desire for instinctual or predatory animal life; it is merely a stronger poetic equivalent for the commonplace metaphor of retreating into or being drawn out of one's shell. Moreover it is an instant flash of feeling that should not be drawn out by elaboration of multiple meanings founded on the life and habits of crabs or lobsters.

From this point on, contemplation of change does not again enter the world of possibility in indicative verbs. No decision is announced; Prufrock merely thinks in subjunctives and then in contrary-to-fact constructions: "Should I ... have the strength...? in short, I was afraid"; and then, "*Would it have been* worth it, after all?" The question of possible action now answered negatively and for good, Prufrock turns to contemplate the twilight existence that such a man as he may look forward to: more of the teas, the white flannel trousers *de rigueur* for resort wear, the thinning hair (never thick), the care of digestion (in 1910 peaches were indigestible, to be eaten with caution). But love is not for him. The smell of hyacinths in spring can recall to him only "things that other people have desired" (*Portrait of a Lady*); he knows love at a distance only, and with its back turned, for the mermaids, as he observes ruefully, are "riding seaward." Below, in the chambers of his silent sea, he may still dream of "sea-girls" wreathing him but they are dreams; the reality of a human relationship he cannot stand: "human voices wake us, and we drown."

The *Love Song* is more than a retreat from love, however; it is the portrait of a man in Hell, though until this truth becomes vividly established in the poem, the hell appears to be merely the trivial one of a self-conscious individual in a sterile society. Prufrock does not analyze himself, and we are not led into peripheral guessing in Freudian or other terms about what may be wrong with him; we simply come to know directly what it feels like, consciously, to be Prufrock. By certain critics the poem has been read with a quite different emphasis, as the ironic picture of a society presided over by ennui. Certainly trivialities abound: proper neckties, "artistic" small talk, and the rest. That is the kind of society in which Prufrock moves, and obviously there is boredom in the empty fullness of its life. Moreover, it suits Eliot's purpose to set the scene superfi-

cially on this level. But within the poem the most individually significant images are of a different order; they are
violent metaphors, out of place if the theme were ennui
alone, even the perhaps deeply felt ennui of a Baudelaire.
The social images are lightly ironic, but these extreme ones
are not; they form a pattern of which the two main
components are objective correlatives for a self-divided
state and a state of paralysis or stagnation. Self-consciousness is a split state: descending a staircase, the
painfully self-conscious man is both himself descending and
those above observing his thin hair; and it is this double
or split consciousness that is the center of his discomfort;
he is simply not all in one piece. Acute self-consciousness,
furthermore, through this division of the self, paralyzes
the will and the power to act and feel, produces "the partial
anaesthesia of suffering without feeling" of which Eliot
speaks, in a different context, in the opening scene of *The
Family Reunion.*

The passage from the *Inferno* which stands as epigraph
to the poem sets the underlying serious tone for *Prufrock*
and conveys more than one level of its meaning: "S'io
credessi che mia risposta. . . ."—lines in which Guido da
Montefeltro consents to tell his story to Dante only
because he believes that none ever returns to the world
of the living from his depth. One in Hell can bear to expose
his shame only to another of the damned: Prufrock speaks
to, will be understood only by, other Prufrocks—the "you
and I" of the opening, perhaps—and, I imagine the epigraph
also hints, Eliot himself is speaking to those who can
understand this kind of hell. "No secret can be told/ To
any who divined it not before," as the author of *The City
of Dreadful Night* also knew. *Prufrock*, I need hardly say,
is not in a literal sense autobiographical: for one thing,
though it is clear that Prufrock will never marry, the poem
(written several years earlier) was published in the summer
of Eliot's own first marriage in 1915. Nevertheless, friends

who knew the young Eliot almost all describe him, retrospectively but convincingly, in Prufrockian terms; and
we know his later view of the dramatic monologue as the
poet's mask. Prufrock was Eliot, with some of the pose
or surface of Laforgue, though Eliot was much more than
Prufrock (more, for that matter, than Prufrock and Laforgue together). We miss the whole tone of the poem,
however, if we read it as impersonal social satire or ironic
portrait only. The "impersonal" theory of poetry to the
contrary notwithstanding, as soon as Eliot found a voice
of his own, the voice was in essence personal; he had not,
in fact, the temperament of a major satirist.

Within the poem, then, are two distinct orders of imagery; there are the limited and literal details of Prufrock's
daily concern, the fashionably combed hair or the stylish
trousers with cuffs; [b] but against these stand out sharply
the extravagant images—highly imaginative and for the
most part violent— and it is through these latter, which
reflect back to the epigraph, that we know we are visiting
a kind of hell. The once notorious opening simile is no
proper description of any evening sky known to man; the
"patient etherised upon a table" indeed extinguishes the
sky, leaving only shock, with the residual thought of illness
and paralyzed faculties, a thought evoked again, less spectacularly, by the stagnant smoke and soot, which are
literal, and the afternoon that "malingers," which is figura-

---

[b] Referred to at the time as "rolled." A trivial detail, but one that
has led to comically ingenious interpretations. Robert Llewellyn solved
the difficulty some years ago in the *Explicator*. We may notice also (near
the end of the Lestrygonians episode of *Ulysses*) that Blazes Boylan was
wearing "Tan shoes. Turnedup trousers." Boylan, too, dressed well.

A reader puzzled by the next line, "Shall I part my hair behind?"
may turn to Conrad Aiken's recollections of the Harvard of his and Eliot's
youth: "An editor of the Advocate had returned from Paris, after a year,
in exotic Left Bank clothing, and with his hair parted behind: it had
made a sensation" (*Ushant*, Cleveland: Meridian Books, 1962, p. 143).
There would be nothing ever seedy about Prufrock, who would go to
his funeral in this year's collar and tie.

tive. Literal and figurative are joined when the trivial self-conscious fear of servants' contempt is universalized into the "eternal Footman's" snicker. The eternal Footman may conceivably be death, as is often supposed, but I do not read the line so; it seems more like the device used for a similar purpose with respect to the woman in the poem, who is never "she" but is abstracted or universalized into "one": "If one, settling a pillow by her head. . . ." It is not this woman only to whom Prufrock will not propose, not this Footman only that he fears: what Prufrock fears, indeed, is not death but life.

More violent images, however, convey the extremes of self-shattering consciousness: "the eyes that fix you" like a specimen insect impaled, to be stared at in its death agony as it ejects its insides at both ends:

> The eyes that fix you in a formulated phrase,
> And when I am formulated, sprawling on a pin,
> When I am pinned and wriggling on the wall,
> Then how should I begin
> To spit out all the butt-ends of my days and ways?

—The most violent image, I think, in all of Eliot but so wrapped in decorum that, neatly managed as it is in the language of a collector's hobby, its force escapes the casual reader. Yet Prufrock is speaking of himself, and what he describes is the abject loss of control of bodily functions in the extremity of agony or terror. Only less violent is the other image of exposure and split consciousness, that of seeing one's own nervous system projected "in patterns on a screen," an image repeated more extravagantly in that of the split self of John the Baptist: Prufrock has "seen" his own head brought in upon a platter. And finally, there is the figure that recalls the epigraph from Dante, just as Prufrock is thinking once more of how it might have been had he attempted to establish an intimacy. "Would it have been worth while / . . . To say: 'I am Lazarus, come from the dead, / Come back to tell you all.' " She

would not understand: "That is not what I meant at all./
That is not it, at all." What have the dead to communicate
that the living could understand?

The doom is real though the tone is dry, kept so by
the absence of direct expressions of feeling, by the trivial
details of social life, by Prufrock's reminding himself that
he is no great tragic protagonist ("I am no prophet," "I
am not Prince Hamlet"), and sometimes by undercurrents
of other allusion, as when the lady's repeated "That is
not what I meant at all" stirs (and very likely was meant
to stir) an egregiously inappropriate echo in one's mind of
Kipling's "rag and a bone and a hank of hair," who "never
could know/ And did not understand," for "it *wasn't the
least what the lady meant.* . . ." The poem is at once both
a highly subjective and a fully dramatic portrait of a young
man who has never been really young and who on the
surface is correct, well-dressed, extremely self-conscious,
a trifle pathetic, and a trifle absurd. Prufrock, however,
knows he is all this, and the acceptance of the knowledge
dignifies him; he is no figure of fun. And there is something
of him, at times, in most of us. In the Prufrockian world,
change, which there means becoming able and willing to
enter into a human relationship through love, is impossible;
the word *love* does not even enter the poem after the title,
and the hell is felt to be permanent.

The Love Song of J. Alfred Prufrock is a finished portrait,
final in more ways than one; for its protagonist there would
be no sequel, only continuance. With his particular kind
of self-respect, Prufrock has accepted the fate of a timid
and solitary temperament; but he will put a good face
on it, will not be a recluse, will always have a proper social
surface. This he tells us. And so, of his author, does Conrad
Aiken tell us, remembering Eliot at Harvard: "He was shy,"
but he went to dances. "He was early explicit, too, about
the necessity, if one was shy, of disciplining oneself, lest
one miss certain varieties of experience which one did not

naturally 'take' to. The dances, and the parties, were a part of this discipline."[1] The young Prufrock, had he required a profession as Eliot did, would no doubt have proceeded to a Ph. D. in philosophy, a dissertation on F.H. Bradley, an academic post at Harvard, teas and cultivated talk in Cambridge; and would have lived the rest of his life *making do*, with a bored, anxious, half-lonely soul.

So Prufrock. It was a "natural" destiny that his author rejected, at some cost. Psychic vitality or, if one believes in it, the genius-will-out law, creative force, the drive that we call ambition, under spur too of an arrogance not evident in Prufrock but evident enough in the young author's various condescenscions—toward the provincialism of his native land, for one thing—in short, all of Eliot that was not Prufrock lured him abroad out of safety into risk, into an emergence which for a time proved nearly calamitous. Eliot abandoned a familiar and secure profession for a job in a London bank, frequented the society of the outrageous Pound, lost a young French friend to death in the war, married Vivien Haigh-Wood (on Pound's encouragement, the second Mrs. Eliot says)[2] in the face of his parents' disapproval. Coming to life, he found within a year or two in his own April, not Chaucer's spring but the cruelest month.

In the years between his marriage in 1915 and the appearance of *The Waste Land* at the beginning of 1922, his poetry was slow in being published or recognized; his wife, as it proved before long, became a hopeless mental (and often physical) invalid; his earnings were insufficient; he himself was seriously overworked and approached physical and emotional collapse. Under these and perhaps other sources of strain he suffered increasingly from what toward the end of this period he described to Richard Aldington as "an aboulie and emotional derangement which has been a lifelong affliction."[3] The "aboulie" I take to be the French version of the psychiatrists' *aboulia* (or *abulia*), a condition

said to be marked by loss of "will power," an abnormal
inability to act: it is Prufrock's anaesthetized evening sky,
his "hundred indecisions" and "hundred visions and revisions" before drinking tea, now intensified by imperative
need for "decisions" and for action.

All this we know, without however knowing or needing
to know all the inner significance—the precise character
of all the relationships involved, the precise weight of each
of the interwoven difficulties. However the causes are
assorted, Eliot's poetry suffered for a time. [c]

[c] In recent years a theory which has gained some currency has purport-
ed to explain both Eliot's private afflictions and certain of the poems,
The Waste Land in particular. In an article of 1952, originally suppressed
under threat by Eliot's solicitors of action for libel but republished since
his death with the support of F. W. Bateson, John Peter traced Eliot's
emotional breakdown to a "close romantic attachment" to the young
Frenchman Jean Verdenal and to grief over the latter's death. Verdenal
lost his life in the Dardanelles campaign in 1915, and when the *Prufrock*
volume was published two years later Eliot inscribed it to Verdenal's
memory with an affectionate quotation from the *Purgatorio*. According
to Peter, this was by no means all. The "dramatic protagonist" of *The
Waste Land*, i.e., Eliot, is still "irretrievably" in love with the memory
of Phlebas the Phoenician, who is also, in symbolic disguise, "the hyacinth
girl" ("they called me the hyacinth girl"): his original "ardour" is still
felt (six years later) as an "insupportable bleakness," and the poem is
in essence a still stunned and grieved meditation upon the irreplaceable
loss of his beloved Verdenal. This, briefly, is the substance of Peter's
interpretation. ("A New Interpretation of *The Waste Land*," *Essays in
Criticism* XIX [1969], pp. 140-175; reprinted, with an added "Postscript,"
from the suppressed version in the same journal of 1952. See also Bateson's
account of the affair at the beginning of the 1969 volume and G. Wilson
Knight's recent argument for a similar interpretation: "Thoughts on *The
Waste Land*," *Denver Quarterly* VII [Summer, 1972], 1-13.) Other writers
have issued broad hints to the same effect.

On the evidence available, I do not know whether Eliot was homosexual (or went through a homosexual period) or not and am unwilling to
make any judgment on the matter. I question anything so strong as
"ardour," simply from what we know of his temperament, and greatly
doubt a six- or seven-years-long broken heart. Even an extremely "close"
emotional attachment seems to me improbable unless it were, possibly,
to his mother—of which a devout Freudian could make something; and
anyone who reads the early poem *The Death of Saint Narcissus* may
have Narcissus for answer. More may come to be known some day, but
for the poetry I do not think it matters greatly. If there was a homosexual

element in Eliot it would seem most likely derivative, not primary. From all we know of the poetry, the prose, the public person, and the published testimony of people who knew him, the foundation of his personality is that of the solitary, the self-sufficient. As such a temperament can scarcely be quite complete in a human being, it may with some such persons give way more easily in relations with one's own kind, one's own sex; or it may not, may instead find in its unlike or complement the partial relief it seeks from inhuman solitude: likeness of sex, that is, may provide a sense of safety or difference be felt as a safe barrier. Because in such a temperament the homosexual element if present is apt to be secondary I do not think the question likely to be crucial for the understanding of the poetry of Eliot. I place this note here, where it belongs chronologically, rather than later, for I am persuaded that Peter's reading throws no light at all on *The Waste Land* but merely confuses us in reading that already complicated poem. If one grants the probability of Peter's premise with respect to Eliot's make-up, the details of *The Waste Land* still cannot be made to fit his interpretation without the most severe wrenching and distortion.

4

The Widening Gyre

> Human voices wake us, and we drown.

The closing words of *Prufrock* are nearly prophetic, and
as a whole Eliot's second volume is not a pleasant one
to read. [a] After the best of the earlier poems these are
a disappointment in both quality and tone, with the partial
exception of the first and last, *Gerontion* and *Sweeney
among the Nightingales.* I half-except also, as in a different
category, the witty satire on the Church, *The Hippopotamus*, reminiscent of Eliot's earlier light satires but more
highly wrought and more substantial, verses written without solemnity by Possum, to which our response should
not be too much colored by memory of the later Anglican
Eliot. Through the rest, particularly the later poems in

[a] For convenience I refer to the new poems of the 1919 and 1920 volumes
as "the 1920 volume," following the classification used later by Eliot in
the *Collected Poems*, although both the original small English and the
American editions actually included the contents of the Prufrock volume
along with the new work.

the volume, those written in 1918 and 1919, a harsh tone prevails, one that repels as the tone of no other of his poems do before or after. Whatever the poet approaches seems to revolt him, not the sordid and false in modern civilization only but the human race itself: the reader finds himself repelled by humanity along with the poet, but also quite separately repelled by the spirit in which the poet writes. Sex is the frequent theme, sex emotionally raw or out of balance, hysterical: subject at its most trivial, in *A Cooking Egg*, to disillusion and at its worst to disgust, as in *Dans le Restaurant* where a common sexual awakening of childhood is seen, degraded, through the talk of a revolting waiter and his revolted, contemptuous, guilt-ridden patron. The poems are ironic and Eliot was already an accomplished ironist. But here the irony is not only dry, it is superior and rather cruel, spiking out in all directions punitively to impale Christian and Jew, obsequious Oriental, middle-American tourist, and the pimpled young "red and pustular/Clutching piaculative pence." Here even the alliteration is an assault upon the reader.

The prime defect of these poems is that for the best satire their victims are all either too easy or too pathetic, and that no self-mockery counterbalances or humanizes a prevailing contempt in the tone. Even the recurrent display of polysyllabic language is insufficiently witty and pointed to seem other than display or than a trivial, slightly sadistic trick played upon the reader. Too rare to have any connotations at all, the polysyllabic words lack such spice or such intellectual pointedness as the superficially comparable scientific term sometimes has in the conceits of a Donne or a Herrick.

Change and development created the pattern and often constituted the theme of Eliot in his next half century of poems and plays. Though his poetry is not, like that of Yeats, running autobiography undisguised, some of it—*Prufrock*, the *Rhapsody*, and the *Portrait* to begin with—is little less deliberately an analogue of such autobiography. This is not true of the poems immediately following the *Prufrock* volume. No verse and no published prose chronicles or recognizably symbolizes the changes that we know occurred: no love poetry tells us what broke the Prufrockian reserve or warmed the Prufrockian heart, supposing it to have been warmed; none records the poet's subsequent troubles. But there is trouble in the overtones of the poems.

SWEENEY AND OTHERS

The title of the English edition of Eliot's second volume, *Ara Vos Prec*, is drawn from the passage in the *Purgatorio* to which Eliot returned more than once later on, "Now I pray you . . . be mindful in due time of my pain" (Canto 26, lines 145-147). Reading the volume, we sense the poet's pain, not embodied where it is constitutive within the poems, but as a disruptive, uncoordinated force distorting their tone. The four poems in French Eliot explained many years later as merely "a sort of *tour de force* to see what I could do." He had written nothing for some time, "was rather desperate," thought he had "dried up completely." [b] The aridity, like the pain, is everywhere evident and like the pain is present mainly to the detriment of the work; it is not, as afterwards it was in *The Waste Land*, creatively objectified or embodied.

In time of drought and emotional frustration, technical exercise and experiment provide an obvious resource, and Eliot saw that even his aridity might be turned into some kind of virtue through technical brilliance. A poet may achieve "a distinguished aridity," he remarked of another poet at the time if "in the inevitable dry times" he is able

[b] *Writers at Work: The Paris Interviews*, pp. 98-99. Pound and Edmond Dulac, Eliot says, assisted with these.

to "master a style." ^c The French verse that Eliot was
trying out is clever but does not represent mastery of a
style; the English quatrains, written during the study of
Gautier that Pound had urged upon him, do have a style,
and they appear to be part of the same effort to stimulate
a more creative vein. In them, Eliot said long afterwards,
"the form gave impetus to the contents."[1] The quatrains
are highly accomplished exercises in wit, confined within
strictly formal limits, moving at a very high speed. Each
poem is compounded of incongruous elements: the urban,
the coarsely contemporary, the contemptible is set without
comment against the romantic, the distant, the cosmic;
Grishkin against the Brazilian "arboreal gloom"; Sweeney
variously against the "unstilled Cyclades," the "stormy
moon" and "River Plate," the "penitential gates/ Sustained
by staring Seraphim"; Burbank against the axle-tree of
heaven and the dawn rising from Istria. The juxtapositions
are Laforguian, partly perhaps still through eyes of
Symons, who had said of Laforgue's prose that, "mathematically lyrical, it gives expression, in its icy ecstasy, to
a very subtle criticism of the universe, with a surprising
irony of cosmical vision." Symons' words describe what
appears to have been Eliot's intention in these poems.

When *Ara Vos Prec* first appeared, in contrast to the
judgment of later readers and for reasons not easy now
to fathom, Eliot passed over *Gerontion* to name *Burbank
with a Baedeker: Bleistein with a Cigar* and *Sweeney
among the Nightingales* as "among the best [poems] that
I have ever done"; they are moreover "intensely serious,"
he said.[2] *Sweeney* is the earlier and the more technically
rigid of these. In the later quatrain poems, rhyme and
rhetorical unit are counterpointed against each other with
the greatest flexibility; in *Sweeney among the Nightin-*

---

^c He ascribed "distinguished aridity" to the current writings of Sache-
verell Sitwell but clearly had himself in mind as well, if not instead
("Contemporanea," in *Egoist*, June/July, 1916, pp. 84-85).

gales, as in the still earlier *Hippopotamus,* rhetorical unit, pause, and rhyme are mathematically exact, and the poem moves forward in spite of, not with the aid of, its form. Of *Sweeney among the Nightingales* Eliot said that "all he consciously set out to create was a sense of foreboding."[3] Accordingly, the danger to Sweeney is undefined—a roadhouse robbery and murder presumably, "nothing personal." The epigraph is Agamemnon's cry of betrayal, "Alas, I am stricken by a mortal blow from within!" With Sweeney are drunken plotting women, his nightingales; there is a "man in mocha brown" with heavy eyes and mouth glittering with gold-capped teeth. Grown suspicious, the man withdraws to look on from outside in cynical amusement through a window incongruously festooned with wisteria, as doom presumably hangs over Sweeney. One is aware that "this sort of thing has occurred before," and down the road the ancient nightingales continue to sing unperturbed in the convent garden. Past and present, neither is to be idealized; and the present is made up of the past. Agamemnon was murdered, though in Aeschylus the nightingales are only a casual simile; they were explicitly present, however, in the sacred wood where Oedipus died. Keats heard the "self-same" song, in illusion the selfsame bird, as Ruth once heard; and Arnold heard the past of Greece in English Philomela. Even her disrespectful "siftings" (Pound's refinement upon Eliot's original "droppings") receive the sanction of history, having earned the approval of Aristotle as a rhetorical device: in the *Rhetoric,* discussing good and bad taste in metaphor, Aristotle had said: "The address of Gorgias to the swallow, when she had let her droppings fall on him as she flew overhead, is in the best tragic manner. He said, 'Nay, shame, O Philomela.' "[d] Sweeney's presumed fate is thus ironically

---

[d] *Rhetoric* III.3 (trans. W. Rhys Roberts). Eliot's year at Oxford, it will be remembered, had been devoted to the study of Aristotle. The identities of Philomela and Procne as nightingale and swallow are interchanged in different ancient versions of the legend.

dignified and universalized through a welter of allusion geographical, historical, legendary, cosmic. *Sweeney among the Nightingales* is a poem not easily forgotten, yet it does not quite live up to its promise; and its failure is due, like that of *La Figlia che Piange*, to the presence of conflicting tones that cancel instead of reinforcing each other. The "forboding," which the imagery tells us should be cosmic, is recognized without being felt because the irony that dictates details of the immediate scene is small-spirited and contemptuous; it is not the large or cosmic irony the foreboding spirit requires, and this forcing together of the two orders of feeling produces rather the effect of a technical trick.

For obvious and unimpeachable reasons, *Burbank with a Baedeker: Bleistein with a Cigar* has been cordially disliked, and it comes as something of a shock to learn that in 1920 Eliot thought this, along with *Sweeney among the Nightingales*, among his best poems and that he moreover described this too as "intensely serious." Returning to it with closer attention after encountering that assertion, one indeed finds it, if not a great deal more pleasant, certainly more substantial, more serious, and more technically remarkable. The earlier poetry of Eliot had been studded with quotation and allusion to myth and the classics, a natural reflection of his tastes and interests. Now, after the experiments in French verse, he evidently set his invention deliberately to work at a new project, the creation of poems which should systematically juxtapose the past and present and finally, in *Burbank* and *Gerontion*, should be virtual mosaics or collages of others' work. Each poem should now be so crammed with allusion, echo, and quotation as to seem made up of little else, yet through ingenuity in combining borrowed materials with minimal additions and alterations, each should make its own statement, create its own mood, wear its own original air. This is very different from the writing of the *Prufrock* period. As Eliot observed at the time,

without reference to himself, it was what Pound too had
been doing of late: "Mr. Pound proceeds by acquiring the
entire past; and when the entire past is acquired, the
constituents fall into place and the present is revealed"[4]
(the two methods were not quite identical, however, for
the ostensible locus of the *Homage to Sextus Propertius*
is the past, that of *Burbank* the present). Eliot's essay
on "Tradition and the Individual Talent" appeared that
same fall, and its relation to the current poems is plain:
the importance of tradition, recognition of the past as
constituting all but the whole of the present, finds objective
proof in the poems, each a small package of pieces from
the past yet each more contemporary than last week's
news.

Eliot once expressed admiration for Henry James's
method, in *The Aspern Papers*, of making "a place [Venice]
real not descriptively but by something happening there,"
and he later said that this was what had stimulated him
to write *Burbank with a Baedeker: Bleistein with a Cigar.*
Whether James would have recognized his offspring is
another matter: the "something happening" in Eliot's
poem is scarcely a story in James's sense. Something more
than thirty allusions and borrowings have been identified
in the twenty-eight lines of this poem and its epigraph;
and if on the one hand a few of the discoveries look like
the product of a critic's imagination, I have no doubt that
more than their equivalent remain unexhumed. They range
from St. Augustine to Spenser, Shakespeare—*Othello,
Hamlet, The Merchant of Venice, Antony and Cleopatra,
The Phoenix and the Turtle*—Marston, and Donne; and
on to Byron, Tennyson, Browning, Gautier, Ruskin (mainly the *Seven Lamps of Architecture*), along with *The
Aspern Papers* itself and further bits of what Burbank's
Baedeker would have pointed out—the Venetian lion and
the horses of St. Mark's, paintings by Mantegna and
Canaletto, frescoes of Tiepolo, and more.

Burbank crossed a little bridge
Descending at a small hotel;
Princess Volupine arrived,
They were together, and he fell.

Defunctive music under sea
Passed seaward with the passing bell
Slowly: the God Hercules
Had left him, that had loved him well.

The poem is generally read as a story, of sorts, in which
"something happens to people in Venice." As Delmore
Schwartz related it (in the *Partisan Review* of 1925),
Burbank finds himself impotent with the Princess Volupine
and has to turn to metaphysics because the contact of
the flesh is unsatisfactory. Meanwhile Bleistein, "A saggy
bending of the knees/ And elbows, with the palms turned
out,/ Chicago Semite Viennese," stares with indifference
at the art of Venice. And Princess Volupine finds a more
rewarding lover in a richer Jew. Read in this way, the poem
is particularly unpleasant and not only because of the
gratuitous insertion of Bleistein, gratuitous because extra-
neous to that particular story. However satirically intended, the picture of Burbank going to bed, or even hoping
to go, with a Venetian princess however shabby, is too
gross for good irony: it shouldn't require all that bludgeon
to demolish poor Burbank. And it helps little to be reminded that the characters are caricatures of types to be met
with in Venice; the point remains on all counts too crude.

The real direction of the poem is slightly different: it
is Venice herself that Burbank falls in love with at first
sight, primed by his Baedeker for his fall. [e] The poem

[e] *"Descending* at a small hotel" is likely to put the reader off, for
it is an odd and rather affected expression for merely arriving in town;
but this is its meaning. By chance recently, I noticed Eliot's employment
of the same idiom at precisely the same time in a prose review: "Henry
Adams in 1858, and Henry James in 1870 (both at still receptive ages),
land at Liverpool and descend [i.e., from one's cab] at the same hotel."
("A Sceptical Patrician," *Athenaeum*, 23 May, 1919, p. 362.)

hangs together and its point is clear if it is read not as
a view of typical persons set against the background of
Venice but as pure satiric allegory. "Meagre" and "phthisic," the Princess Volupine is of course but only incidentally
the attenuated shadow of Browning's Venetian lady, she
of the "superb abundance" of breast in *A Tocatta of Galup-
pi's*, which is quoted in Eliot's epigraph. That contrast
is subordinate; centrally she is Venice herself personified,
Queen of the Adriatic now reduced to phthisic princess:
Volupine, still voluptuous though emaciated, now vulpine
too in the poverty of her decay, preying in a small way
upon the Burbanks but selling and letting her palaces to
the Sir Ferdinand Kleins. It is what we see, with all its
difference of method and tone, in *The Aspern Papers* but
earlier in Spenser more explicitly. In *The Ruins of Time*,
which furnishes Burbank's concluding reflection, Spenser's
Princess was the city itself: "I was that Citie [the ruined
city of Verulamium]." "I of this small northern world [in
Roman Britain] was Princesse," says the symbolic lady
of the visions—herself personifying "time's ruins"—to
Spenser's poet. The focus of Eliot's satire is equally that
ruin of time the Venice of today and modern attitudes
toward it in Burbank's provincial, uncritical eagerness to
admire what is only the "smoky candle end of time" that
still "declines," leaving no more hope of profit even for
Shylock's descendent Bleistein—"On the Rialto once," we
are reminded. The piles on which the city stands are rotted,
rat-infested; Venice has long since fallen to the money-
lenders: "The Jew is underneath the lot" (Pound's
usura?). [f] The Shylock type of Jew, having now moved
on for profit to the fur business, is replaced by the other
caricature-stereotype, the newly-rich social-climbing Sir

[f] Mrs. Eliot finds Pound's handwriting in suggestions for revision of
a preliminary draft of the poem, though not with reference to *usura* or
Bleistein. *The Waste Land: A Facsimile . . . of the Original Drafts* (*WL
Facs.* hereafter), p. 131.

Ferdinand Kleins, to whom the phthisic Princess-city will
sell anything.

Burbank is the best of the lot. At least, he is allowed
to reflect at the end, with his own innocence but through
his author's witty, not innocent, rewriting of Childe Harold,
who even in his day was mourning at much greater length
the already advanced decline of the city, not forgetting
her symbolic lion:

> St. Mark yet sees his lion where he stood
> Stand, but in mockery of his wither'd power,
> Over the proud Place where an Emperor sued,
> And monarchs gazed and envied in the hour
> When Venice was a queen with an unequall'd dower.

Eliot takes the wind neatly out of Byron's rhetoric, and
Venice brings no dower to Burbank in spite of his readiness,
as he reflects:

> Who clipped the lion's wings
> And flea'd his rump and pared his claws?
> Thought Burbank, meditating on
> Time's ruins, and the seven laws.

The worship of dead tradition was not what Eliot was
preaching that year in his essay on "Tradition," and in
a broader sense what the poem satirizes are false romantic
values in worship of the past; it is these to which Burbank
succumbs and which sap his strength. Reading *Burbank
with a Baedeker* in this sense, we can understand why
Eliot should have called it "intensely serious," and can
even recognize some basis for his regarding it as highly
as he did, at least while it was hot off the fire. For while
by its technique it is keeping the past alive by saying
something contemporary through its means, in theme it
presents the obverse of the living use of tradition, for its
theme is that of tradition dead, the dead corrupted Venice
herself sliding into the sea to the "defunctive music" of

the passing bell, a corpse that is yet speciously held in
honor by the sentimentalism of Burbanks and Baedekers.
As a mosaic, the poem is an extremely brilliant *tour de
force* in the workmanship of which Eliot must have taken
pleasure, as the reader cannot help doing also, in spite
of which it remains slightly distasteful, for its virtuosity
is ostentatious, its tone contemptuous, its anti-Semitism
more than casual. Swift's hatred of mankind was not what
the "healthy" would call healthy, but its world of values
is one that we share or can imagine sharing. The hostilities
we feel running through the "Burbank" poem and indeed
throughout this volume of Eliot are at the edge of that
world and at times outside it. Such poems as these raise
the old, still grave question of an acceptable relation
between the ethical or the human and the aesthetic.

One other short poem is worth attention but only in
passing and not for its poetic value, an "Ode" which
appeared in *Ara Vos Prec* but not in the American edition
of 1920 or in any later collection and which, it is said,
Eliot never allowed to be reprinted. A distillation of the
mood of these years, the "Ode" is impenetrably murky,
and murky evidently by design, with a theme built around
Catullus's marriage song (Number 61) and employing its
refrain, "Io Hymen, Hymenaee," with the Catullian "boys"
transformed into children "in the orchard." The poem is
not a celebration, however, but a malediction—upon someone or something—epitomized in its epigraph from
Shakespeare's *Coriolanus*. In the play, among the few
half-propitiatory words uttered by Coriolanus are words
spoken when he goes over to the Volscians:

> My name is Caius Marcius, who hath done
> To thee particularly and to all the Volsces
> Great hurt and mischief.
>   [IV. 5. 71-73]

In Eliot's epigraph these lines are decapitated and so
transformed into a malediction: omission of the first line
leaves the remainder imperative or optative:

>   To you particularly, and to all the Volscians
>   Great hurt and mischief.

The poem is clearly intended to be private and had best remain so except as its evident mood confirms that of the other poems, supposing there has been any doubt about it, the mood showing through Eliot's attempt, in the absence of creative impulse and in the midst of unmastered personal difficulties, to produce poems by pure force of will, ingenuity, and intellect.

GERONTION

The important poem in the volume of 1920 is assumed to be *Gerontion*. Looking forward to *The Waste Land,* it supplies a link in the development of Eliot's handling of structure in the longer poem, though nominally it is a dramatic monologue like *Prufrock*: scarcely more than nominally. In *Gerontion* Eliot abandoned the conventional support of narrative and dramatic elements altogether. What is retained is only a single speaker characterized by old age, decrepitude of body and mind, rootlessness, "a dull head among windy spaces" in a rented house, inheriting not so much as a ghost. The speaker projects no action, contemplates no decisions, reveals no character; he is merely there. He is in short an exceedingly generalized persona, the mere ghost of a human being; and the person to whom he speaks, if present at all, is even dimmer, a ghost's ghost. "I that was near your heart"—the presence of any "you" is momentary and intrusive, for Gerontion is even more solitary than Prufrock. Prufrock as a person had been the center of his poem; Gerontion is primarily an abstract seeing eye. They share the curse of aridity, but Gerontion's is mainly that of age on one level and on another that of an era; in Prufrock the aridity is mainly his own, with incidental glances at his society, for his theme is himself. Nevertheless, without the individualized Prufrock's at all entering into the later poem, his presence, and Eliot's behind the scene, is implied through two key quotations and allusions, both now well known.

The opening quotation is taken almost verbatim from A. C. Benson's biography of Edward FitzGerald, whose *Omar* had been a great discovery of Eliot's adolescence. "Here he sits, in a dry month, old and blind, being read to by a country boy, longing for rain." Many years later, sketching for a Harvard audience the early development of his taste, Eliot described the chance discovery of *Omar* when he was fourteen or so and the "almost overwhelming introduction to a new world of feeling which this poem was the occasion of giving me. It was like a sudden conversion; the world appeared anew, painted with bright, delicious and painful colours." [g] The bright colors are doubly faded, for Eliot and the aged FitzGerald. There was a Prufrockian side to FitzGerald himself, however, as we see him in Benson's book; though gentler and more evidently affectionate, he was another of those who dwell on the fringes of life and so has his submerged place in the generic persona of Gerontion.

The other major source of imagery is *The Education of Henry Adams*, which Eliot had recently reviewed in the *Athenaeum*. As Hugh Kenner has observed, the Adams of Eliot's review is "a wealthy Prufrock;"[5] and so is the Adams of the autobiography itself. Born an insider in his society, Adams was never more than an outsider in life; he is less "ridiculous" than Prufrock believes himself to be, but he may be in some respects less admirable: at least Adams complains more; all that is lacking for him in life he traces to the world—to the failure of his "education"—and only now and then perfunctorily to himself. Prufrock knew better. The language of Adams breaks into

[g] *The Use of Poetry and the Use of Criticism*, p. 25. As Benson's biography was not new (it was fifteen years old when *Gerontion* was written), Eliot may have gone rather out of his way to weave his private tribute into the poem.

the surface of the poem as if by chance, through his
puritanically half-shocked delight in the lush bloom of a
Maryland spring:

> The Potomac and its tributaries squandered beauty. . . .
> Here and there a negro log cabin alone disturbed the dog-
> wood and the judas-tree, the azalea and the laurel. The
> tulip and the chestnut gave no sign of struggle against a
> stingy nature . . . profligate vegetation . . . intermixture
> of delicate grace and passionate depravity that marked the
> Maryland May. [h]

Selecting and compressing, Eliot transformed Adams's
ambiguities of mood to serve his own purposes.

The detached, floating series of allusions, names, reflections on history that make up most of *Gerontion* may be
meant to look like the "free association" that preoccupied
many psychologists at the time; that at least seems implied
in the concluding lines,

> Tenants of the house,
> Thoughts of a dry brain in a dry season,

---

[h] *The Education of Henry Adams*, the opening of chapter XVIII.
In view of remarkable comments made on this passage and symbolic
meanings assigned to it in conjunction with Eliot's use of it in *Gerontion*,
by critics evidently unfamiliar with trees of eastern North America, it
may be well to mention that dogwood (Cornus florida) is not a "weed"
but a familiar and much-loved small spring-flowering tree, a distinctive
feature on the edge of woods and in cultivated gardens; the flowering
judas (Cercis canadensis), also known as redbud, is another spring-bloom-
ing tree; the laurel is the beautiful native flowering shrub Kalmia latifolia,
unrelated botanically and in connotation to the European laurel, its chief
attraction being its spring flowers; the tulip is another handsome tree,
and the chestnut the native American kind (now extinct from blight but
common in Adams's day and in Eliot's youth), with flowers less readily
describable as phallic than those of the European or horse chestnut. These
were all as familiar to Eliot as to Adams. Eliot's distortions of nature
are present (partly present in Adams as well) but are much less pronounced
than many readers have argued. For those familiar with the dogwood
in bloom, some little effort is required to think separately of either "dog"
or "weed."

which close the poem as it opens, with the imagery of drought. As one reads, the thoughts of Gerontion appear to proceed through a phantasmagoria of random images and names in a succession that approaches chaos. It is not chaos, however, nor is it pure "mood" like the earlier *Rhapsody on a Windy Night*. For, floating along on mood, one encounters at the center a rock of rational statement and suddenly realizes that the succession of images is not at all "free." Phantasmagoria though its parts are, a symmetrical structure of blocklike units takes the place of chronology, descriptive continuity, or stream of consciousness, to create a form different from that of any earlier poem. Like *Burbank*, *Gerontion* is crammed with allusions and borrowings, though they are not quite so thickly strewn. For the most part they come in larger blocks, are more intricately interwoven into a central statement, and become more fully submerged in the texture of the poem. The result is far more complex than anything Eliot had previously attempted.

Gerontion himself is an abstract Prufrock with a difference not of age and individuality only: the First World War has intervened, and he is primarily man at a moment in history, is, in fact, the mind, the old age, of Europe in 1919. At the center of the poem stands a judgment of history, which seems to have behind it Shelley, Yeats, and Henry Adams in his role of historian, possibly even Spengler, though *The Decline of the West* had appeared in its German form only the year before and had not yet been translated.

> History has many cunning passages, contrived corridors
> And issues, deceives with whispering ambitions,
> Guides us by vanities. . . .

With all that history has to teach, Gerontion's reflections continue, we are defeated by our own weakness and her ambiguities. Man's virtues have spawned his vices; conversely, the virtues themselves were forced upon him by past crimes. History's lesson comes too late, is not believed, or not believed passionately enough.

This has a familiar ring. "Mere anarchy is loosed upon the world," Yeats had written a few months before:

> The best lack all conviction, while the worst
> Are full of passionate intensity. [i]

And Eliot had just then been reading in *The Education of Henry Adams* that "History's truths are little valuable now"; what historians, priests, and evolutionists "affirmed or denied in 1860 had very little importance indeed for 1960. Anarchy lost no ground meanwhile." These and other similar statements occur in the chapters in which Adams is writing as a professional historian.[6] A century before, after the close of an earlier "world" war, Shelley had described the Europe of his day in Yeats's own terms, as both Yeats and Eliot very likely remembered:

> The good want power, but to weep barren tears.
> The powerful goodness want: worse need for them.
> The wise want love; and those who love want wisdom;
> And all best things are thus confused to ill.
>
> > (*Prometheus   Unbound*, I, 625ff.;
> > written   in   1818- 1819)

Eliot ends *Geronion* as Yeats begins *The Second Coming*, with the whirling gyre of destruction, "Turning and turning. . . . Things fall apart."

---

[i] *The Second Coming* had been written but not published before Eliot wrote *Gerontion*. He may have seen it in MS, through Pound or otherwise, but we do not know that he did, the parallels, therefore, though striking, may be accidental. For the date of Yeats's poem, see Ellmann's *The Identity of Yeats* (N. Y., Oxford, 1954), p. 257. A good account of Eliot's changing views of Yeats is that of Ellmann in the chapter "Possum's Conversion" in *Eminent Domain* (New York, Oxford, 1967).

De Bailhache, Fresca, Mrs. Cammel, whirled
Beyond the circuit of the shuddering Bear
In fractured atoms. Gull against the wind, in the windy straits
Of Belle Isle, or running on the Horn.
White feathers in the snow, the Gulf claims,
And an old man driven by the Trades
To a sleepy corner.

Eliot's imagery of destruction is nautical and planetary but essentially the same and almost equally cosmic, since the "Trades" (a name not derived from the "trade" of commerce) are part of the great planetary air currents associated with the earth's rotation; after "gull against the wind," ship "running on the Horn," planetary winds are intensified into cosmic hurricane to "whirl" De Bailhache, Fresca, and Mrs. Cammel in widening gyres

Beyond the circuit of the shuddering Bear
In fractured atoms,

for the center no longer holds.

Gerontion thus ends with the foreseen collapse of Western civilization, as it opens, in a loose metaphorical sense, with a crisis nearer Europe's beginning. The Greek stand against Persian hordes from the East at Thermopylae (the Greek word for the "hot gates" of Eliot's third line) becomes an implied parallel to the war of 1914, seen as Western civilization withstanding the Germanic hordes and, by 1919, threatened by impending hordes from the Russian East. Nor can Western man be saved by his religion, which perhaps was doomed from the start.

The central passage on man's failure to learn from history is symmetrically enclosed between parallel, antithetical paragraphs on Christianity. In the first, Christ the tiger comes in the life-stirring spring; but the spring itself is morally diseased—"depraved May"—and today's participants in the sacrament of Communion, in which Christ

is "divided," "eaten," and "drunk," are themselves lost,
mere names, without identity, of a rootless European
decadence, whose participation in the Christian sacrament
is without meaning or efficacy. In the corresponding paragraph that follows the rejection of history as a teacher,
the sacrament is reversed: "us" Christ devours. Whether
Eliot meant it so or not I am not sure, but the line may
imply what Yeats implies, again in *The Second Coming*,
the "twenty centuries of stony sleep . . . vexed to nightmare"
by the birth of Christ, the Kaiser's "Gott mit uns" having
climaxed all the old religious wars and having met its defeat
only months before Eliot wrote. The hopes of Christianity
have failed, and the theme now, by implication, becomes
the abstract one of value in general.

> Think at last
> We have not reached conclusion, when I
> Stiffen in a rented house. Think at last
> I have not made this show purposelessly
> And it is not by any concitation
> Of the backward devils.
> I would meet you upon this honestly.
> I that was near your heart was removed therefrom
> To lose beauty in terror, terror in inquisition.

This passage, the poem at its most obscure, preludes
the final statement of destruction. It has been subject to
varying and conflicting readings, with some critics, perhaps
wisely, taking refuge in a recital of sources and allusions.
I am not confident of my reading, but, speaking tentatively,
the passage appears to me one in which Gerontion represents on different levels the personified decrepitude of
Europe in 1919, and also, under the figure of old man,
the author both as author and as private person. As the
generic old man he knows that the end of the gyre, the
"conclusion," will be after his time, that the theme is

broader than one man's age. But this also is a partial transition to the next lines, which I read as the author's assertion that, appearance to the contrary notwithstanding, he has not been writing nonsense in his phantasmagoria, is not cheating the reader with false prophesies of doom, and is not merely facing backwards into history to read the secrets of the future:

> I have not made this show [read "poem"] purposelessly
> And it is not by any concitation
> Of the backward devils.

These devils have been recognized as augurers and diviners in the *Inferno* (XX) who having presumed to foretell the future were condemned to walk forever backwards, heads reversed on their shoulders, tears pouring down their rumps. The poet, then, is protesting his sincerity, "I would meet you upon this honestly," and his apparently acrobatic poem is not mere clowning as in virtually pre-Joycean 1919 it might have been thought. The lines anticipate a more ironically phrased declaration at the end of *The Waste Land*: "Hieronymo's mad againe," but Hieronymo was not mad and would fit the play to the characters more truly than they could guess: the poet inversely defending his poem.

At this point in *Gerontion*, however, Eliot injects what is phrased as a purely personal statement, one for which no reading has been found that properly sinks it into the fabric of the poem. He takes lines from Middleton's *The Changeling* (lines he quoted with admiration in a later essay on Middleton),

> I that am of your blood was taken from you
> For your better health,

and rewrites them into a very different kind of statement:

> I that was near your heart was removed therefrom
> To lose beauty in terror, terror in inquisition.

The difficulty is owing largely to the insertion at this point in *Gerontion* of an extravagantly emotional statement in a highly personal tone, for nothing of which is there outward basis in the rest of the poem, where aridity, not emotional intensity, prevails. In their sound and their abrupt violence, breaking out among the thoughts of a brain too dry, really, for such intensities, these lines suggest something breaking out from a layer of feeling that has little to do with the persona of Gerontion. It is a fine-sounding passage in itself, but it has no context. The "you" has been variously identified—with FitzGerald, with Eliot's wife Vivien, with some anonymous fictitious presence in the poem, with God; it could also be the poet's mother, or his father, who had died earlier in the year. The choice doesn't really signify—and that is the real weakness of the passage—because none of these identifications will successfully place the lines in the poem: if Eliot had a rationale for their presence, the rationale was too deeply concealed to count. Under whatever interpretation one chooses, "terror" and "inquisition" are outside the scope of the poem, for even the decline of the West is seen only in the nonhuman terms of fractured atoms; yet "near your heart," "terror," and "inquisition" are precisely what Eliot went out of his way to add to Middleton.

Apart from certain overtones, the surface of what follows consists of the old man's description of his loss of passion, of potency, of the keenness of all his senses; his language, however, suggests both the larger theme, the decay of civilization, and the aridity which is the poet's as well as the old man's. One holds off chaos and death with "a thousand small deliberations," one hopes to prolong the life of the senses by artificial stimulants; but these devices do no more than "multiply variety/ In a wilderness of mirrors." The variety is illusory, for there is no escape in what prove mere fragments and distortions of the reflected self. Eliot was remembering and half reversing a passage

from Pound's *Near Perigord* III, which he had quoted twice
not long before:

> And all the rest of her a shifting change,
> A broken bundle of mirrors . . . !⁷

There is no escape, either, for civilization, because history
too affords only variety in a wilderness of mirrors; it reflects
only ourselves, our self-deceptions: ultimately, no escape
is possible from the gyre that widens into chaos "beyond
the circuit of the shuddering Bear."

The greatest weakness of *Gerontion* is the breaking into
its surface of the passage "I that was near your heart,"
with its "terror" and "inquisition," the greatest weakness
because it is made to sound so important yet is not only
intellectually obscure but impossible to reconcile with the
rest in tone and feeling. There are minor obscurities,
however, and minor misjudgments deriving from what
seems unresolved emotion. *Prufrock* had represented a
man's accommodation to what is, after exploring fruitlessly
what might be. In *Gerontion* there is no real acceptance
of what is; neither is there any projection in hope or even
in wish or imagination of an alternative; its world, despite
its talk of history and its manifold allusiveness, has the
air of a personally boxed-in present. The spirit flails about
in vain, is persecuted and persecutes the reader with a
gratuitous goat's cough overhead and with all that is
implied in "spawned," "blistered," "patched and peeled."

Among the minor misjudgments, as it seems to me, is
Eliot's staking too much on a series of proper names. The
partakers in Communion are named, faintly characterized,
geographically or culturally placed: "Mr. Silvero . . . at
Limoges," "Hakagawa, bowing among the Titians," "Madame de Tornquist" in a seance, "Fräulein von Kulp . .
. in the hall"; and these figures are symmetrically balanced
in the block structure of the poem by the uncharacterized
De Bailhache, Fresca, and Mrs. Cammel. The names are

all, no doubt, as they are said to be, invented, and their
sound may half suggest some connotation or other; but
whatever they may have meant to Eliot, the reader's
associations aroused by them are insufficiently controlled
by their context; and if associations are lacking altogether,
as they may be, the names fall dead or send the reader's
mind scrambling for vain answers.

Eliot's intention may
have been to refine upon the old dramatic tradition that
created the Sir Giles Overreaches, or Corvino, or Peregrine
a Gentleman Traveller, for he was reading intensively in
the Elizabethan and Jacobean dramatists at the time; but
apart from primary differences between poem and play,
the old names, simple convention though they may have
been, had sure, controlled, and limited associations; they
meant something and the same thing to everyone and
meant not too much.

In *Gerontion*, however, the names distract or intrude,
or both. And I am afraid that in my own case something
else intrudes: Betty Foy and her Idiot Boy (who laughed
for joy, and so on) and, almost in the same class, the
lugubrious heartbreak of a refrain manufactured by another poet out of a name, "Luke Havergal, Luke Havergal."
The remark is unfair to Eliot; but still the absolute
individuality of a proper name makes it extremely ticklish
to handle. In *The Waste Land* the momentary "Stetson!"
presents no problem: he is an ejaculation, the name of
a hat, any good hat (we should always have known, as
we know now definitely from Mrs. Eliot, that Stetson could
not be the raffish figure of Pound, could indeed be no
individual at all).[8] "J. Alfred Prufrock" is fine, suggestive
enough and individual enough; "Gerontion" also is perfectly representative and no more; both are judiciously kept
out of the text and, above all, are not invented for the
sake of an easy rhyme, as one fears of Betty Foy. The
succession of names in *Gerontion* is no such egregious
blunder, but it does, I think, represent a minor lapse of

judgment as to what constitutes a viable objective correlative.

To return, however, from this small spree on names. As work on this second volume of poems was being concluded in the fall of 1919, the two celebrated critical essays "Tradition and the Individual Talent" and "The Problem of Hamlet" (later "Hamlet," in *Selected Essays*) made their appearance. Though issued and received as general pronouncements of poetic doctrine, they represented less the philosophically trained aesthetic thinker Eliot than the particular T.S. Eliot of the moment, who had been writing these poems of 1918-1919—as the author finally informed his readers in terms only less specific, after having hinted as much for many years. "In my earlier criticism," he said in the lecture "To Criticize the Critic," "both in my general affirmations about poetry and in writing about authors who had influenced me, I was implicitly defending the sort of poetry that I and my friends wrote"[9] ("My friends" may be in part a matter of urbane tone in the lecture, for no friends, not even Pound, were writing quite the "sort of poetry" contained in that year's volume).

Aside from the obvious connection between the critic's emphasis upon tradition and the poet's use of multiple allusion, the two essays associate themselves even more specifically, "Tradition and the Individual Talent" with the shorter poems (*Burbank*, the *Sweeney* poems, and one or two more), "Hamlet" with *Gerontion*, the distinction lying in what the two essays and the two groups of poems do with what had now become a problem, the place of emotion in poetry. Eliot did not propose to ignore it in a theory of art; yet his thought wavers, and though the essays coincide exactly in time, "Hamlet and His Problems" appearing in the *Athenaeum* in September 1919 and "Tradition and the Individual Talent" in the Septembr and December numbers of the *Egoist*, they are not perfectly consistent in the values they assert or imply. The "Tradi-

tion" essay makes, on the one hand, a generalization which
should be the classic correction for all hasty critical emphasis upon "intensity of emotion" in poetry: "It is not
the 'greatness,' the intensity, of the emotions, the components, but the intensity of the artistic process, the pressure,
so to speak, under which the fusion takes place, that
counts." But in promulgating his "Impersonal theory of
poetry" in that essay Eliot goes as far as he can toward
brushing off emotion altogether. Great poetry may be
"composed out of feelings solely," he says, without "emotions," leaving the difference between feeling and emotion
undefined; moreover, "emotions which [the poet] has never
experienced will serve his turn as well as those familiar
to him," he adds without qualification and with a shade
of contempt in the expression "will serve his turn." Finally,
the essay asserts that "poetry is not a turning loose of
emotion, but an escape from emotion"—distinctly a rhe-
torician's, not a logician's, pair of alternatives; and in so
begging the question, the critic turns away from the answer
his own "objective correlative" in the other essay had given
him.[10]

Except for *Gerontion*, the poems of this date stand out
as the most deliberately "impersonal" of all Eliot's poems;
they represent an "escape" that is rather like a flight from
emotion, unless we take them to be deliberate expressions
of a general spirit of detestation for which any object will
serve. They are not this; they are primarily escapes through
intellectual interest in technical innovation, intermittently
marked, however, by exhalations, through rifts, of emotional frustration and half-randomly directed detestations.
Gerontion is somewhat different from the others. In it Eliot
is not consistently lashing out and is not escaping from
emotion entirely into technique. Unlike what he said of
emotion in the essay on Tradition, his account of the
objective correlative in the "Hamlet" essay neither dis-
misses nor minimizes emotion but asserts that in order

to "express" it in poetry the poet must find "a set of objects, a situation, a chain of events which shall be the formula of that particular emotion." *Gerontion* may have been written with the theory of the objective correlative specifically in mind and with consciously chosen correlatives for some part at least of its author's emotional state. The weaknesses of the poem seem a reflection of imperfect control and imperfect crystallization of those emotions, and a reflection also of indecision about what he wished to reveal and what to conceal. Perhaps knowingly, Eliot faced the same problem he ascribed to Shakespeare in the essay: *Hamlet* is an "artistic failure," he said, because the circumstances of the story are inadequate correlatives for Hamlet's—and behind Hamlet Shakespeare's—emotional state. Eliot too had "tackled a problem which had proved too much for him." [j] In a way that affects the entire poem and not one passage only, he was trying to create in the composite structure of *Gerontion* the objective correlative of an experience or state of mind in which the emotion "exceeded the facts" of the poetic situation or differed too greatly from those "facts" in kind and in tone of feeling. Europe in 1919 might have produced a poem of despair or disgust, but the despair and disgust in *Gerontion* are not primarily of this kind; there is a personal something else that tastes bitter on the tongue and that is not adequately objectified in the thought or the language of the poem. And so the goat coughs overhead when it needn't and when there is no goat.

Eliot already had in mind, however, another work, a long poem.

[j] *Selected Essays* pp. 145-146. On the precise date of composition of *Gerontion* there is conflicting testimony. Mrs. Eliot (*WL Facs.*, p. xvi) refers to it as completed by 25 May, B. L. Reid (*The Man From New York*, New York: Oxford University Press, 1968, p. 405) calls it "an important new poem" on 29 September (this would be a few days after the essay was published). Both dates are based on letters of Eliot to John Quinn. Whatever the specific dates of writing, the poems and theories obviously developed together and in relation to each other.

5

The Waste Land

Civilization is hooped together, brought
Under a rule, under the semblance of peace
By manifold illusion; but man's life is thought,
And he, despite his terror, cannot cease
Ravening through century after century,
Ravening, raging, and uprooting that he may come
Into the desolation of reality.

W. B. Yeats, *Meru*

Encrusted as it is with tradition nearly as much from
without as, in a different sense, within, *The Waste Land*
has to be dug out afresh by every reader. For many years
now, Eliot's most celebrated poem has been attended by
an accretion of stories, some encouraged by the author
himself: stories of the shock caused by its appearance, of
the notes' being an elaborate joke or, alternatively, of their
having been written merely to fill up pages, or worse, to
send amateur detectives off in vain pursuits; stories of the
poem's being itself largely a joke and of its being precisely
the opposite, a savage attack upon women or, even

Eliot's heartbroken *In Memoriam*; stories, too, of a lost
manuscript proving Pound to have been the *de facto* author
by virtue of a ruthless blue pencil. As late as 1966, so
eminent a critic as Wilson Knight, plausibly enough, with
the *Cantos* in view, was denouncing the presumed result
of Pound's assistance: it is "clear," he said, that Pound
was responsible for the discontinuities, the "fragmentary"
structure or absence of structure, which had left the poem
defective.[1] Of these questions, something hereafter. For the
time being, I disregard the legends in favor of the poem—so
far as I make it out—as it stands in itself and in relation
to the whole of Eliot's poetic history.

THE POEM AS PRINTED

Technically, *The Waste Land* is a development from
Burbank and *Gerontion* in a direction that bestows fuller
meaning upon the technique itself. In theme, different as
it both looks and is, it descends from *Prufrock*. Its canvas
is no longer confined to a single figure; poetic range and
technique approach the opposite extreme as microscope
gives way to cinemascope. The terms of its central question
are different and the answer is different, yet at its most
abstract level, *The Waste Land* again asks the question:
now, for human beings of the modern world and not only
for the Prufrocks, is change possible? In contrast to *Prufrock*, the answer at the end, after the Thunder has spoken,
is (as I understand it) "perhaps." There are uncertainties
in the conclusion, uncertainties of chronology, with the
order of events and tenses of verbs shifting back and forth
bewilderingly. The life-giving rain appears to have come,
yet at the end the land is still arid, London Bridge still
"falling down," and the message of the Thunder—*give,
sympathize, control*—still I think hortatory rather than
achieved. Nevertheless, the end does clearly suggest possible hope.

Leading to that equivocal answer is the question itself,

posed in concrete terms under the implied, universalizing rubrics of earth, air, fire, and water. Of these elements, three are alluded to directly in the titles as well as in the imagery of the main divisions: "Burial of the Dead," with its "earth" covered in "forgetful snow" and the embedded roots of the opening, its "handful of dust," and its corpse planted in the garden; "The Fire Sermon," with its sequence of the fires of lust and its double allusion to the fire sermon of Buddha and St. Augustine's confession of youthful lust in Carthage, "Burning burning"; "Death by Water" with its drowned sailor.

The second of the elements, air, is absent from the final title of Part II, "A Game of Chess," which replaced an earlier one, "In the Cage," the latter possibly too pointed in allusion to the scenes of persons trapped in sexual relationships. Too pointed perhaps also in alluding to James's story of sorry sexual frustrations *In the Cage*, which like Eliot's scenes—with James's "merciless clairvoyance," as Eliot once called it[2]—juxtaposes high life and low life, impassably separate. As "air" it may have alluded also to the poem's epigraph from Petronius (supposing this to have been already chosen): the Cumaean Sybil in her cage, hanging in air, wishing for death. Whatever reason there may have been for the changed title, the element of air is prominent in the imagery: in the odors of perfume "stirred by the air/ That freshened from the window" and in the dialogue:

"What is that noise?"
        The wind under the door.
"What is that noise now? What is the wind doing?"
        Nothing again nothing

—a passage which reminds one (as it may have been intended to do) of Joyce's windy palace of Aeolus, the newspaper office. The whole of "A Game of Chess' is insubstantial talk, and Eliot as well as Joyce must have

remembered Chaucer's knowing piece of science, that sound
"is noght but air y-broken,/ And every speche that is spoken
. . ./ In his substaunce is but air." All the elements are
brought together at last in "What the Thunder Said." [a]
Under this universalizing schema, then, the present world
—"the immense panorama of futility and anarchy which
is contemporary history," as Eliot described it a year or
two later[3]—is anatomized in the four divisions of the poem
preceding the Thunder's message. Can life grow out of such
stony rubbish as the poem presents? Reduced to its simplest terms, this is the theme of *The Waste Land*.

Certain features of the poem, however, and they are those
that once appeared most novel, are employed in the service
of a quite different idea from that of possible change or
rebirth: an idea inherited most directly from Matthew
Arnold, whom Eliot had been rereading, concerning the
loss in modern times of a "unity of culture" such as once
blessed the world, or at any rate as much of the world
as then seemed to matter, Western civilization. Eliot, and
before him Yeats and Pound, owed more to Arnold than
they were sometimes disposed to acknowledge and in particular, I think consciously, owed to him much of their
formulation of the idea of tragic loss suffered by the
breaking apart of that "bright girdle" once furled about
the world, the "sea of faith." These three poets are in their
different ways the true Sons of Dover Beach. Their solu-
tions, when they had any as Eliot had after his accession
of faith, were different from Arnold's when he had any,

---

[a] I do not wish to make too much of this aspect of the poem's structure.
It is incidental to the theme, and Eliot does not mechanically restrict
each class of image to its assigned division; in particular, there are allusions
throughout, for obvious reasons, to water or the absence of it. His structure
somewhat resembles the much more rigid, smaller-scale structure of
Shelley's *Ode to the West Wind*, where leaf, cloud, and wave each takes
its turn to dominate but together are cumulative, each caught up and
translated, sometimes forcibly, into the imagery of the next, with, in the
end, all recapitulated together.

but they all took from Arnold that central idea and they all, in consequence, felt responsible in their role as poets for serving as bearers of tradition and unifiers of culture. The Essay on "Tradition" had already shown something of this preoccupation. Though Eliot's lifelong admiration was for Dante and probably in time he came to see certain of his own poems as, in distant parallel, his own *Inferno*, *Purgatorio*, and *Paradiso*, that analogy was in the nature of a tribute rather than of attempted rivalry; he never was and never thought himself to be quite the modern Dante. On the other hand, he did deliberately set himself, as I think, in prose as well as poetry to become Arnold's rival, successor, and improver. Partly also under the influence of Pound, he succeeded ultimately in becoming Arnold's successor as a fountain of certain kinds of critical ideas. And in *The Waste Land*, on one level, what are all the quotations and allusions doing but carrying out literally Arnold's injunction to know and propagate "the best that has been known and thought in the world," demonstrating the relevance of the past to the present, exemplifying the value that a unified broad culture may have in giving power to what one has to say (and, in passing, showing its author equipped, as Arnold believed the critic if not also the poet should be, with knowledge of more than one's own language and literature)?

Gerontion, *Burbank*, and other poems of 1918-1919 had constituted a preliminary flourish in this direction; but they do not suggest that Eliot had yet quite thought out all the implications of the poet's responsibility as he shortly came to see it. In those earlier poems any allusion, however casually chosen, would do providing it could be worked in; the interest lay in the dazzling ingenuity of the construction, and sources consisted of whatever came to hand that would fit, whatever book Eliot was reviewing at the moment or whatever allusion to Venice he could think of, whether in itself it had much value or not. This is not

to say that the poems were pure rag-bag magpie work.
In *The Waste Land*, however, the choice of sources is
always principled, never random; what Eliot draws on now
almost without exception is the main line of our cultural
inheritance or, less frequently, what he thinks should be
part of the main line (as in his use of the *Pervigilium
Veneris*). As poet, he is making himself responsible for the
continued or revived life of past values; from which it
follows, too, or should follow, that the sources and connotations of the allusions themselves enter into the substance
of *The Waste Land* more fully than they do in the
preceding poems. Those had more often approached the
technique of the collage, in which what happens to have
been printed on the bit of pasted newspaper is irrelevant
to the picture. *The Waste Land* has little of the collage
in this sense.

In one of its primary aspects, then, *The Waste Land*
is a going demonstration, really an exhibition, of an ideal
unity of culture, and was surely meant to be so. This is
one important reason why, in addition to its central
concern with the theme of death and rebirth (the specific
form that significant change so often took in Eliot's
thought) Jessie Weston's *From Ritual to Romance* was
so much to Eliot's purpose, for in developing its theme
that book traces one unifying, significant archetypal myth
through many forms and many cultures and ages; it too
in its different way was demonstrating the unity of culture.

"Unity of Culture," however, provides not the theme
of *The Waste Land* but its method or technique, one
assisted into being also, no doubt, by the example of the
cinema's kaleidoscopic handling of time and space, as well
as by certain aspects of Pound's and the Symbolists' poetry,
and of *Ulysses*: London metamorphosed into ancient
Rome; the living dead crossing London Bridge on their
way to work in Dante's city of the lost dead; failure of
romance in the hyacinth garden sandwiched between pas-

sages of romantic love, first of hope, then of despair, from
Tristan und Isolde; the modern lady of the boudoir distantly recalling Pope's Belinda as well as Shakespeare's
Cleopatra; Tiresias foreseeing the dreary seduction of the
typist. Though, as his theme requires, the present suffers
in the comparison—a currently popular song, the "Shakespeherian rag," is scarcely Shakespeare and it may be
thought unfair to set Lil in the company of Ophelia—still,
Eliot is no Miniver Cheevy, does not wholly romanticize
or urge a return to the past. On the contrary, he takes
care to remind us of brutal lusts of the past in Tereus
and the violation of the Rhine maidens, and of the sorrows
of Tristan as well as the delights of Spenser's "Sweet
Thames" daughters. Other times and places mingle with
the present throughout the poem essentially as a *technique*
conforming to an ideal unity of culture, while thematically
the poem pursues its course, develops its own statement,
poses its own question: Is there hope for civilization? how
can it be saved? what is it now, that it should need saving?
"What are the roots that clutch, what branches grow/ Out
of this stony rubbish?"—the immediate rubbish in these
lines at the beginning being fragments of futile talk heard
or overheard in the Hofgarten, where the bored and the
displaced of Europe put in time, living in the past, denying
their identity ("Bin gar keine Russin, stamm' aus Litauen,
echt deutsch")—"A heap of broken images. . . ." [b]

b The lines having to do with "Marie" and her cousin the archduke
derive from the Countess Marie Larisch. George L. K. Morris ("Marie,
Marie, Hold on Tight," *Partisan Review*, 1954; reprinted in *T. S. Eliot*,
Twentieth Century Views series, ed. Kenner, 1962, pp. 86-88) drew attention to her book *My Past* as a source for this and numerous other passages
in *The Waste Land* but I think exaggerates its influence apart from the
"Marie" lines. Some of the parallels which he draws I did not find in
reading the book, and others seem far-fetched or uncertain. The Countess's
lively book does, however, offer by implication its picture of contemporary
European decadence. The present Mrs. Eliot reports that Eliot had met
the Countess herself and had been told by her about the sledding (*WL*

At the end of the poem, these unfertile fragments of the present are replaced by other "fragments" of positive value out of the past, some of them of hope, hinting of renewed life: Arnaut Daniel in the refining fire of Purgatory; the *Vigil of Venus* with its message of a spring that may not be cruel, "Tomorrow shall be love for the loveless"; and the more equivocal fragment from Gérard de Nerval's *El Desdichado*, "I am the dark, the widowed, the disconsolate," the Prince of Aquitaine in the ruined tower, who has crossed Acheron *twice* ("Are you alive, or not?" the lady of Part II asks; and one recalls the allusion to Lazarus in *Prufrock*). These are significant "fragments" suggesting Arnold's "touchstones," which the speaker has "shored against his ruins." But the answer to the poem's question of what the modern world can do to be saved is not "unity of culture," it is "DA"—of which more in a moment.

The subject is society, but not society conceived as a system; and it is this latter circumstance more than its sporadically inserted personal elements that places *The Waste Land* properly in the sequence that begins with *Prufrock*: for the ills of even the public world are not represented here as curable by any change in its public institutions of church or state, not by social, economic, or political means. The illness is of the sum of individual souls, as in *Prufrock* it is of one representative soul; and its cure can be wrought, if at all, only through ethical and emotional change in those souls. The formula for this is "DA"—"*Datta*" (give), "*Dayadhvam*" (sympathize), "*Damyata*" (control, especially self-control), the choice of words from the Sanskrit being logically (whether or not poetically) justified by the fact of their representing the ancient linguistic link between East and West and so symbolizing the unity of culture at its broadest, while their

Facs., pp. 125-126). Lines 12-18 are usually read as a single conversation. To me they seem better read as bits and pieces, with only the four lines in the middle read as continuous speech; though the difference is trifling, fragmentation is part of the point.

substance advances the main theme of possible salvation for the waste land of the world through change in the individual. [c]

Eliot's picture of the world is both unified and universalized by the recurring imagery of drought, of city superimposed upon city, river upon river, and by the variations played upon the theme of sexual failure or distortion, episodes and imagery that nearly all reflect the emphasis of Jessie Weston's study of the Grail myth. Though the insistent emphasis upon the sexual may well have originated, as many readers now suppose, in Eliot's marital problems, concentration on the sexual as symbol serves the particular, less personal ends of the poem by focusing the ills of the modern world within the context of the individual soul and out of reach of socio-political questions: sexual episodes spring from lust or boredom, running the gamut of seduction, rape, homosexual solicitation, all without love; romantic love is unfulfilled, marriage fruitful where the fruit is unwanted. In this second major poem, then, the question again ultimately concerns subjective change dependent upon the individual. *The Waste Land* does not actually explore change; even Prufrock, imaginatively projecting what the impossible experience would be like if he could undertake it, comes closer to doing this. Yet the poem expressly looks toward some alternative to Gerontion's whorl of fractured atoms.

Are we, however, in the face of certain disclaimers of Eliot, entitled to ascribe to *The Waste Land* such large meaning and to take it as seriously as all this? Milton

---

[c] Buddhist and Hindu influences on *The Waste Land* have been discussed recently in the columns of *TLS* (May 1973). Though of interest in themselves the questions raised seem to me of only minor significance with reference to the thought of the poem. As one of the disputants has implied, *The Waste Land* is an English poem; it is not mystical, not Hindu, and not Buddhist. The virtues subsumed under DA are humanist virtues, whatever their language.

would justify the ways of God to man, but Milton was
not troubled by self-directed irony. Would the ironical Mr.
Eliot, with

> his mouth so prim
> And his conversation, so nicely
> Restricted to What Precisely
> And If and Perhaps and But,

have permitted himself this wide flight upon a theme
almost comparable to Milton's, directed toward an ethical
and psychological salvation of the world? the theme of
a world waiting for spiritual rain in a landscape of Unity
of Culture? Is this possible, when even the author himself
has put the poem down as a mere piece of "rhythmical
grumbling"? The answer is nevertheless yes, it is possible.
And first because it is all clearly there in the poem, much
of which can be explained by nothing less. Moreover,
however modest his manner could sometimes be, Eliot was
never hesitant about saying large and wide things in his
prose. Within a few years of *The Waste Land* he would
be saying even larger things, with a confidence not inferior
to Milton's.

Eliot's inclination to belittle, afterwards, what he had
attempted in *The Waste Land* is not surprising. His
conception of an appropriately polished manner on the
lecture platform or elsewhere, with its *pro forma* depreca-
tory mask—itself the inverse side of arrogance warring with
a residue of shyness—would have encouraged such a tone;
but the initial reception of *The Waste Land* may have
prompted it in the first place. Eliot was no more indifferent
than most writers to the reception of his work, and as
a rule his response to criticism was not, like Pound's,
defiance. He had staked a great deal on the poem; it was
highly wrought, and it was his first really long poem. Yet,
with few exceptions, immediate public reaction was unfavorable, and unfavorable in peculiarly galling ways. Only

a few early readers seem to have praised the poem: Pound
knew its importance as soon as he saw it—"about enough
. . . to make the rest of us shut up shop," he said;[4] and
after its publication in 1922, the *Dial*, under John Quinn's
prodding, awarded Eliot its prize for the year. Conrad
Aiken, another old friend, reviewing it with qualified praise
in the *New Republic*, called it "important" and "brilliant,"
and described it as "a powerful melancholy tone poem." [d]
Good friend that he was, however, even Aiken could find
little else to say that was favorable; and in any case, Pound
and Aiken, the *Dial* and the *New Republic* were not then
the literary establishment; and Eliot, critical though he
was of its taste, was not one to relish its scorn; he could
not blow it away with a blast like *Hugh Selwyn Mauberly*
and stalk off to Paris. He would have liked approval from
the establishment—on his terms, not theirs—and this he
did not receive, though as an already valued contributor
to the *Times Literary Supplement* he had reason to hope
for favorable or at worst respectful treatment there.

When it came, however, the review in the *TLS*, though
acknowledging excellence in Eliot's earlier work, was severe. Whoever its author may have been (so far as I know
he is still anonymous), he either knew Eliot personally
or knew a good deal about him and obviously knew of
his recent breakdown. In the poem, "we seem to see," the
reviewer wrote, "a world, or a mind, in disaster and mocking
its own despair." He saw nothing at all to praise in the
poem: most of its best lines were borrowed and the whole
was mere parody "without taste or skill"; "some unsympathetic tug has sent Mr. Eliot's gift awry," he concluded.
Other reviewers were equally severe: F.L. Lucas found the
"parodies" "cheap" and "the imitations inferior," at the
same time guessing that the whole poem might be "a

[d] As a whole, the review suggests friendship more strongly than admiration. (It is reprinted in Tate, *Eliot*, pp. 194-202.)

theosophical tract," which is to say, "fantastic mumbo-jumbo."[5] Accusations of obscurity or ostentatious display of learning—even, from the prudish, of indecency—the author of the poem might have expected and put up with unperturbed, but he could scarcely have been prepared for the charges of mere tasteless borrowing, "cheap" parody, and second-rate imitation.

The notes were not spared either. They were thought "pedantic," pretentious, and useless to the "poetic critic" (*TLS*). It is in this context that we read Arnold Bennett's report of a conversation which gives some indication of what had become of Eliot's hopes for the work within two years of its appearance. At that time evidently respecting Bennett a good deal, Eliot had called upon him for advice on another matter, and Bennett's Journal (for 10 Sept., 1924) records the visit:

> I said to him: "I want to ask you a question. It isn't an insult. Were the notes to *The Waste Land* a lark or serious? I thought they were a skit." He said that they were serious, and not more of a skit than some things in the poem itself. I understood him. I said I couldn't see the point of the poem. He said he didn't mind what I said as he had definitely given up that form of writing. [e]

The gradual reversal of critical opinion left Eliot a decade later still somewhat cynical on the subject. The poem was iconoclastic; he had no wish to have been the spokesman of "a generation," expressing its "disillusionment." Neither would he claim it as "an important bit of social criticism": to him it had been "only the relief of a personal and wholly insignificant grouse against life; it is just a piece of rhythmical grumbling."[6] But he had had the poem, or

---

[e] *Journal* (New York: Viking, 1933), p. 786. Eliot had earlier begun "feeling toward a new form and style" (letter to Aldington, 15 November, 1922, *WL Facs.*, p. xxv). He now sought Bennett's advice about dramatic writing, evidently meditating what later became *Sweeney Agonistes*.

whatever it grew out of, seriously in mind for a number of years.

THE WORK IN PROGRESS

Eliot spoke very differently of *The Waste Land*, at precisely the same time as one of his disclaimers appeared, in his essay on Pascal, where he wrote of it with the utmost seriousness under the shelter of impersonal syntax. There, without naming it, he described the composition of "What the Thunder Said," the key section of the poem, as a creative experience that had been almost mystical. In the essay he had been speaking of a single religious mystical experience in the life of Pascal, who was not, as Eliot emphasized, temperamentally at all a mystic (any more than he himself was); the experience had come to Pascal during a period of severe ill health. "It is a commonplace," Eliot continued—and according to Mrs. Eliot we have his word for the fact that he was now describing his own experience in writing the final climactic division of *The Waste Land*—

that some forms of illness are extremely favourable, not only to religious illumination, but to artistic and literary composition. A piece of writing meditated, apparently without progress, for months or years, may suddenly take shape and word; and in this state long passages may be produced which require little or no retouch. I have no good word to say for the cultivation of automatic writing as the model of literary composition; I doubt whether these moments *can* be cultivated by the writer; but he to whom this happens assuredly has the sensation of being a vehicle rather than a maker. No masterpiece can be produced whole by such means; but neither does even the higher form of religious inspiration suffice for the religious life; even the most exalted mystic must return to the world, and use his reason to employ the results of his experience in daily life. You may call it communion with the divine, or you may call it a temporary crystallization of the mind. Until science can teach us to reproduce such phenomena at will, science cannot claim to have explained them; and they can be judged only by their fruits.[7]

Much of this is said again two years later, and parts of it are amplified, in the "Conclusion" to *The Use of Poetry and the Use of Criticism*.

As Eliot describes the experience here, his ill health was the condition that had freed his creative power but not the subject of what he had written. This is the first point to be observed; the second is that he is far from treating the poem either explicitly or by implication as mere rhythmical grumbling, or as "mere" anything. Whatever he may have said in the offhand ironies of a public lecture, the poem was serious enough to have been meditated "for months or years," was finally completed through a crystallization that might be called inspiration and that in 1931, even after his religious conversion, he dared speak of within the context of Pascal's great religious experience. "What the Thunder Said" survives, as we now see from the manuscript, very nearly as originally written, with only the most minor revisions. It is the key division of the whole poem: "not only the best part, but the only part that justifies the whole, at all," Eliot wrote to Bertrand Russell, who had praised it.[8] The greatest service of the now celebrated revisions lay in bringing the rest of the poem into clearer harmony with its conclusion; and as the reputation of *The Waste Land* grew, Eliot's tendency to disparage it in public may possibly have owed something further to the discomfort of knowing how much assistance from another poet this most celebrated of his works had required. He was nevertheless invariably punctilious in acknowledging its debt to Pound.

Eliot had had a long poem at least vaguely in mind since 1916 or earlier: the rhythmical grumble had thus been brewing for some five years. In those times, however,

any but a narrative poet had to get over the obstacle of
Poe's well-known dictum that a successful long poem is
impossible. Pound had already set out on the Cantos
explicitly defying Poe, and Eliot's later critique of Poe's
doctrine outlines his own conception of what the long poem
may be. Poe had held that, as a high pitch of emotional
intensity is essential to poetry and as intensity cannot be
sustained through many lines, a good poem must be short.
The method Eliot had already devised for *Gerontion*, of
joining block to block often without discursive or chronological continuity, had already foreshadowed one way of
neutralizing Poe's dictum, and in the much later lecture
"From Poe to Valéry" (1948), he took specific exception
to Poe's assumption that, as he put it, "the whole of a
poem had to be in one mood." He argued for a more
capacious poetic form in which "a variety of moods,"
requiring "a number of different themes or subjects, related
either in themselves or in the mind of the poet," can form
"a whole which is more than the sum of the parts." Certain
passages in such a poem may even "show no lustre when
extracted," he said, "but may be intended to elicit, by
contrast, the significance of other parts." As for Poe's
"intensity," a long poem may even "gain by the widest
possible variations of intensity."[9] By the time Eliot wrote
this, the *Quartets* had been written, but it is *The Waste
Land* first of all that is being defended and that answers
most fully to his description.

Eliot's ambiguous kind or degree of poetic unity still
disturbs certain of his critics. Is *The Waste Land* one poem
or many? Is—or are—the *Preludes*? *The Hollow Men*? Is
Ash Wednesday one poem or six? the *Quartets* one or four?
We treat *The Waste Land* as one (there should be no
disagreement about this), and Eliot referred to it almost,
but not quite consistently as "a poem." Pound, who at
the time knew it better than anyone else, called it *a* poem
in writing advice to Eliot, but subsequently described it

as "a series of poems, possibly the finest that the modern movement in English has produced," and elsewhere as "a very important sequence of poems." Perhaps the question is capable of solution only by arbitrary fiat; for who knows, really, when a group of dance tunes becomes a suite or a suite a sonata? Sonatas exist which from the standpoint of "organic unity" might better have been called suites, but no one minds. The arguments originate from our ingrained Coleridgean notion of organic form tracing back largely to Aristotle's preference for the dramatic over the looser epic form and afterwards rendered sacred by infusion of the Neoplatonic "One." [f]

Eliot's characteristic way of working—"doing things separately and then seeing the possibility of fusing them together, altering them, and making a kind of whole of them," as he described it[10]—was facilitated by the exceptional homogeneity of his work, a homogeneity originating no doubt in limitations of temperament but capable also of being turned to advantage. Other considerations aside from Poe influenced the form of *The Waste Land*, in particular the problem of avoiding extended descriptive passages in a poem not primarily narrative, while still finding place for the concrete spatial world; and the way had been prepared by his mosaic poems of 1917-19. The form of *The Waste Land* is similar, planned on a larger scale, greatly refined, and with the blocks of literary quotation and allusion now interspersed with passages of monologue taken more or less directly from life, in contemporary speech high and low, the whole fabric remaining throughout a structure of blocks within blocks, the significance of each dependent on its clear relation sometimes to

[f] In addition to Pound's letters of the period, see Robert Langbaum in Litz, *Eliot*, p. 96. There is far more to the question than this; but insistence upon absolute classifications does not seem to me in keeping with what we actually find and experience in art. This is not the place to pursue that complex question, however.

neighboring blocks, always to the whole, and all steadily moving towards the final voice of DA: Shall I at least set my lands in order? Though it is late and London Bridge is falling down, one may then at least hope for rain, and spring.—Eliot was a master of that elusive thing we call "movement" in verse; it rarely failed him even when his chosen structure, as in mosaic, would seem most recalcitrant. Without that mastery, *The Waste Land* would have been less *one* poem than it is.

The "lost" manuscript of *The Waste Land* with Eliot's revisions and the more famous ones of Pound, upon which, during its absence from view, more than one theory had been built, was at last discovered and made available to the public in Mrs. Eliot's facsimile edition of 1971. The manuscript (actually, for the most part, typescript) is illuminating in several ways but confirms few of the earlier speculations. In particular, it puts to rest the supposition that Pound was responsible for the "fragmentary" form of the poem, that he had wrecked its continuity. There had been no continuity, in this sense, to be wrecked; and nothing resembling a transitional passage had anywhere been excised.

The surviving typescript of the version shown to Pound does not appear to be quite the Ur-text; what survives does not reveal the growth of the poem from its inception in any such completeness as does the most remarkable record of the kind that I know, Yeats's series of drafts, from a prose sentence or two, to the final "Byzantium" poems. The revisions of *The Waste Land*, recorded as we now have them, represent mainly a work of excavation: "Ezra performed the Caesarean Operation"—so ran a line of jocular verse in Pound's subsequent letter to Eliot, and on the whole he was right. The operation shows the essential, serious poem in the process of being lifted out into clarity. And the revisions seem also to have completed a process of change, already in essence complete, from the original plan of the poem. What that plan was we do not know, but as it appears to have been well advanced by the end of 1919, it must have differed significantly from the one finally adopted, for Jessie Weston's book *From Ritual to Romance*, which is now integral to the poem—as Eliot said, it suggested "not only the title, but *the plan* [my italics] and a good deal of the incidental symbolism"—was not published till 1920. The Weston material had all been incorporated into the poem before the present typescript came into existence.[11]

Eliot's original working title is no bad starting point for a look at the matrix or the nearest that we can come to the matrix: "He do the Police in Different Voices." Old Betty Higden, in *Our Mutual Friend*, boasts of her foundling son Sloppy's accomplishments: "Sloppy is a beautiful reader of a newspaper. He do the Police in different voices." By this, we seem to be promised technical experiments in a variety of styles, moods, voices, including ventriloquy of low life, and are offered one of several keys to the poem's structure and so to the author's answer to Poe's doctrine. As the title, even the working title, for a long-meditated serious poem, however, it can suggest at best only such remote, satirical seriousness as the earlier *Burbank* and *Sweeney* poems afford; and the poem at this stage does open in some such manner, with fifty lines of narrative in what sounds like Sweeney's own coarse voice, describing a drunken night out, a visit to a brothel, an encounter with a Policeman. Ultimately, Sweeney's night out was sacrificed, apparently by Eliot himself rather than Pound, and is not missed.

So far as the record goes, Pound's excisions and written comments are exclusively directed to the quality of the individual passages: "Too much tum-pum at a stretch," "diffuseness," and "Il cherchait des sentiments pour les accommoder a [*sic*] son vocabulaire," he writes in the margins; but the more significant effect of his and Eliot's revisions seen as a whole, a consideration that one imagines must surely have been present to both their minds, is the transformation effected in the prevailing tone and the formal unity of the poem (an effect almost the reverse of what Wilson Knight speculatively ascribed to Pound's services). Sweeney's "couple of feelers down at Tom's place" and their sequel had blocked what now stands as the serious opening of the poem; with their removal, "April is the cruellest month" and what follows is at once related in theme, key, and tone to the close, "What the Thunder Said," with its unbroken seriousness.

A second, even longer passage originally opening "The Fire Sermon" in the parodied voice of Pope, with "Fresca's" morning ritual replacing that of Belinda in *The Rape of the Lock*, was cancelled on Pound's pointing out that "you cannot parody Pope unless you can write better verse than Pope—and you can't."[12] Pound might have mentioned Joyce as well, for in that passage, remembering Leopold Bloom, Eliot had sent Fresca to the bathroom in Popeian couplets; the wit falls short. Pound was right; but in addition, and the quality of verse and satire aside, the long parody had opened "The Fire Sermon," like "The Burial of the Dead," on what for the final poem was a discordantly trivial satiric note. The deletion of Fresca's eighty and more lines brought to the opening the perhaps newly written passage which again strikes the true note for the desolate waste land. "The river's tent is broken"; there is no rustle of summer leaves as "the wind/ Crosses the brown land, unheard." Now, with *unheard* marking the silence of the leafless trees as well as the absence of the city "nymphs" who have departed, the poetic tone is set firmly enough to take in the modern nymphs as well as Spenser's, absorbing into its mood even the litter of cardboard boxes and cigarette ends that follow.

The third major excision from the poem (an omission that Eliot seems to have somewhat regretted) left only the final ten lines of "Death by Water" in Part IV. Here, as we see it in retrospect, the difficulty had been not so much that of a trivial tone, though the tone and style are unsure and extremely uneven; it was a question, rather, of cutting out a narrative of shipwreck in which the theme was out of keeping with the poem as a whole, for *The Waste Land* is not concerned with the ways of God to man (punishment by shipwreck) but with man's self-involved fate. The narrative was an excrescence in other respects as well: it was too specifically American and nautical for a poem whose main scene is London and too strikingly complete an episode to be readily absorbed into the larger fabric. In itself it is an intense narrative, spoken in the voice of a dead Ulysses recounting his final post-Homeric voyage: a blend of Homer's, Dante's, Tennyson's Ulysses, of Conrad's narrator in *Typhoon* and the Ancient Mariner with his visions and his biscuit-worms, and with more than a shade of Masefield here and there in the writing, all translated to the fishing banks of the North Atlantic on a voyage setting out from Eliot's remembered Cape Ann and the Dry Salvages, and ending with the fatal Arctic ice barrier "dead ahead."

In spite of its inconsistent tones and occasional grotesque insertions, the strain of personal feeling in this narrative suggests that to the author it had some importance; it might even have symbolized the drift towards death from which at the time of writing he was already recovering and which he could by this time partly but not sufficiently objectify. The individual intensity of the episode as well as its narrative completeness obtrudes if we try to read it as part of the longer poem; and though it is the most interesting of the excluded passages, it was clearly both inferior and irrelevant. As "Death by Water" now stands, whether Phlebas the Phoenician has drowned by shipwreck, war, or suicide is immaterial; he belongs to the ritual of the drowned god-king who may be reborn, and he thus provides a transition to Part V; he represents the fourth of the Heraclitean elements, water; he unites in cultural history the ancient and the modern Semite Mr. Eugenides, with whom he is connected by what may be the longest-distance pun in literature—his bones picked in whispers by "a current under sea" foreshadowed by the otherwise superfluous currants in the pocket of the Smyrna merchant.

Though nothing of the sort is recorded in the published correspondence or in comments on the typescript, the sum of the excisions and revisions suggests that after Eliot had written his inspired final section "What the Thunder Said," both he and Pound saw that the essential poem, not the conclusion only but most of the earlier part as well, for all its variety of tones and its alternations of lyrical and satiric passages, was more straight, more severely and directly serious in its prevailing tone than perhaps it had started out to be. The revision excavated what *The Waste Land* had now become (I should think knowingly but possibly only half so). [g] In the final poem all the divisions begin and end in a serious "poetic" tone: even the somewhat inferior Cleopatra (or Cleopatra-Dido) opening of Part II, in spite of its "period" versification, is neither satire nor parody, and the seriousness is now distinct and firm enough to absorb the contrasting episodes, even those of Lil and the carbuncular young man.

A consistent dominant tone, then, in keeping with the theme, and, in the most indefinite sense, a single point

[g] It seems possible that an early plan, never quite taking shape, may have projected a large-scale satiric poem focused upon London as *Burbank* had been focused upon Venice, written in the multifarious voices in which London can speak now or in the past; but the character of any such hypothetical poem had already changed before the existing MS and typescript came into existence. Hugh Kenner's conjecture is of a poem on London "perceived through various Augustan modes" (Litz, *Eliot*, pp. 34-35) with "The Fire Sermon" as its center, and this too seems a possibility for the plan at a still earlier stage.

of view in the end unify the poem. Technically, however, there is no single persona, no single narrator or protagonist. *The Waste Land* is not a dramatic monologue like *Prufrock* or even nominally one like *Gerontion*; critical attempts to make it so result in excessively strained readings. The tonal control is more subtle, is not anchored in any presumed speaker or in any named figure within the poem though there is a gesture toward this in Tiresias. "We" and "me" and "I" and "you" are generalized and shifting. Sometimes they are Eliot, a distanced Eliot (or his persona if one insists on that shibboleth), or Eliot half-identifying himself with Tiresias or the Fisher King; but sometimes they are clearly not. In this waste land we are all in a like state: the pronouns do not matter.

The influence of Percy Lubbock's *The Craft of Fiction* tended for some years to chain our critical imaginations to the requirement of a technically identifiable, and usually single, "point of view" both in poetry and in prose fiction, but there is no such rigid law or rule in the actual practice of writers. Even James, who was highly conscious of the functions of technical point of view, maintained no such invariable, schematic rigidity. In *The Waste Land*, unless we have set out with a foot rule to look for it, we do not even notice, nor should we notice, the shifting "I," "we," "you." Eliot's note on Tiresias tells us that Tiresias is "the most important personage in the poem, uniting all the rest" and that what he sees "is the substance of the poem." This I suspect may have been a slight *ex post facto* overstatement arising from nervousness about the poem's formal unity. Nevertheless, as a mythological personage Tiresias is a naturally symbolic figure for the theme: he who has been both man and woman has been all things and can know all things. And Eliot's poem *is* its question and answer concerning the universal, or at least Western, future. The identity of all the men and all the women, however, to which Eliot's note points, is only broadly symbolic; it has to do with the theme and with unity of culture, not with any narrow consideration of technical point of view or "narrator" or with one specific protagonist concealed behind a series of masks. We hear the voice of the author, who is, let us say, his own persona in a generalized sense, in most of the serious poetic passages that imprint their character upon the whole poem; we need no explicit narrator residing within it.[13]

Returning to the question of Eliot's disclaimers concerning the subject of *The Waste Land*, we may be agreed that in writing the poem Eliot was not looking upon himself as spokesman for a generation, disillusioned or otherwise. The spirit of the early 1920s was not one of widespread disillusion; and the poem is not, in any case, a spokesman's poem. Obviously, it springs from a state of mind and a personality. Prufrock was an arid man, Gerontion was waiting for rain; Eliot had spoken of his own aridity. The imagery of drought in *From Ritual to Romance*, with its double symbolism of individual and general sterility, provided the unifying symbols needed; and in fact even the English weather cooperated that year. Literal drought surrounded Eliot, for 1921 was the rare year in England in which no rain fell for six months, Richard Aldington tells us in his autobiography: "The sun shone every day, and the green fields of England were burned brown, while shrubs and even trees wilted and died."[14] Eliot was in serious psychological trouble and feared his creative vein had "dried up," yet he could no longer be satisfied with the "distinguished aridity" of those acrid poems of 1918-19. Parts of *The Waste Land*, as we know, derive from personal experience or direct observation, and the temptation is to read the poem as pure personal allegory: to find in "April is the cruellest month" not a reversal, for society, of Chaucer's spring but a difficult marriage or the difficult recovery from a breakdown marked by "aboulie"; to find the same allusion in "Are you alive, or not?" and the double crossing of Acheron by the Prince "à la tour abolie" (not quite "aboulie," but nearly so); to find this breakdown itself in "Death by Water," particularly in its original form describing shipwreck; finally, to see the hope of recovery as the Fisher King waits at the end; and to see, further, some sort of autobiography in several (if not all) of the sexual episodes. [h]

The temptation has to be resisted, nevertheless, for one reason that is plain from the face of the poem: no such reading will work as the exclusive or even primary level of meaning because it leaves out too much of the poem and in particular turns too much of the "unity of culture" material into an unrelated, arbitrarily imposed cross-pattern. It makes pretentious nonsense out of such lines as "Jerusalem Athens Alexandria/ Vienna London," and of a great deal else as well. If, as Eliot tells us in his notes, Tiresias is its central figure, an autobiographical reading requires that he be somewhat personally T. S. Eliot, a presumptuous claim. The double sex, according to some theories, might be supposed to do, but for the poet to present himself through the ancient and archetypal figure of prophecy and human omniscience, merely in order to describe his own private troubles, will not do; it reduces the poem to bad construction and worse taste.

Many of these personal correspondences are present, legitimately so since the author is not excluding himself from the waste land; but within the poem they are sufficiently transformed to take their place as illustration or instance, not as theme: they provide the poet with part of his concrete, and felt, material. Eliot's poem is no Wordsworthian *Prelude*, however disguised; neither is it

[h] From notations on the typescript it is apparent that the dialogue of "A Game of Chess" is in some degree autobiographical; and the monologue of Lil's friend, Eliot said, came from the Eliots' maid (*WL Facs.*, pp. [10]-[11], 127).

his *Lycidas* or an analysis of a nervous breakdown. *The Waste Land*, in sum, reveals—or betrays, if you will—its author's "grouse against life," but its subject is something else. Shakespeare may have seized upon the Hamlet story in part for obscure personal reasons, as Eliot's essay on the play suggested: the story may have furnished an objective correlative (inadequate, Eliot argued) for a state of mind. But the story is *Hamlet*; its subject *is* objective; and so is *The Waste Land* in this sense. The arid man sees an arid world, his eye is selective and to that extent distorts the world; but it is still the world that he represents, not allegorical autobiography. Knowing some of the origins and circumstances of composition of the poem does mainly one thing for the reader: it sharpens his perception of the tones and undertones that are present in the finished work. To the reader of perfect sensibility and attentiveness the knowledge would be superfluous; but such a reader can only be poetically imagined.

One transmutation of the personal deserves particular notice. A line in the original version, the most intimate, possibly, in the whole of *The Waste Land*, was removed before publication, evidently for personal reasons, at the request of Vivien Eliot. Without it, the conclusion of the Cleopatra scene as published has always been unsatisfactory, for the passage that provides the final title for Part II, "A Game of Chess," has never slipped naturally into its context. Puzzled, we have gone dutifully where Eliot's note sent us, to the game of chess in Middleton's *Women Beware Women*, and have returned only the more puzzled if now able to disguise our mystification by talking about Middleton. With the missing line now supplied from the original typescript, the passage does more than fall perfectly into place; it casts its shadow significantly back over all the scene, coloring with sadness what without it has seemed a more superficially felt frustration:

> And we shall play a game of chess:
> The ivory men make company between us
> Pressing lidless eyes and waiting for a knock upon the door.

The second line of these three deserves to be reinstated in the established text.[i] Chess may be competition, or war between two, or relief from boredom; here, as the restored line makes certain, it is a futile bridge, and a futile barrier also, between two solitudes: " 'Speak to me. Why do you never speak' "; and to the spoken " 'I never know what you are thinking,' " the reply is unspoken, "I think we are in rats' alley." The implications of the ivory men are further underscored if we know Eliot's earlier use of the line. All three, as well as a number of other scattered images, were lifted from "The Death of the Duchess," which Eliot never published but which went to Pound along with *The Waste Land* (it is now included in the *Waste Land Facsimile*). In that poem a separate line carried the meaning of the scene to its roots: "But it is terrible to be alone with another person."

Even as the poet sat in contemplation before the aridity of the world, his own—to judge by the tone and style in which he speaks—is partly dissolving.

> What are the roots that clutch, what branches grow
> Out of this stony rubbish? Son of man,
> You cannot say, or guess, for you know only
> A heap of broken images, where the sun beats,
> And the dead tree gives no shelter, the cricket no relief,
> And the dry stone no sound of water. Only
> There is shadow under this red rock,
> (Come in under the shadow of this red rock), . . .

---

[i] The fact that the line was not canceled in the surviving typescript and the further circumstance that some years after Vivien's death Eliot himself restored it from memory (in a fair copy of the poem made for a benefit sale) might properly be regarded as authorizing its return to the official text. See *WL Facs.*, pp. [12]–[13] and Mrs. Eliot's note, p. 126.

The brittle, determinedly unromantic style that had characterized the earlier poems with only brief and rare departures, has ceased to be Eliot's hallmark. He is now writing with some of the deeper sonorities and incantatory formulas of the biblical prophets (his notes refer the reader to Ezekiel and Ecclesiastes): "Your shadow at morning . . . /your shadow at evening"; "I will show you . . ./ I will show you fear in a handful of dust." "Your altars shall be desolate, and your images shall be broken," Ezekiel says: and Eliot now proved to have a fine ear for this deeper-toned style: for the syntax that is parallel but not too parallel or too long continued in its parallels, and for the satisfying cadence that brings to a close these sequences; for the concrete universals also, of which much of the imagery consists.

It is a risky style, as we know from Whitman, all too easily imitated when a mere change of the "tell-tale" article can transform *a* cricket into *the* (generic) cricket, a universe of crickets—a device which could even, without much absurdity, have universalized weevils in the sailors' biscuits (like the fly in the ointment) into "the weevil in the biscuit," which is a remark about life, not weevils. I use for this figurative language the term concrete universal—not in its philosophical sense, concerning which anyhow I am a trifle vague—but because the two words, taken simply, describe most exactly the particular rhetorical use of singular substantives that are concrete but unspecific, and so very unspecific as to be all-inclusive (if the rhetoricians have another name for this, I do not know it). As a formal costituent of style, it is most familiar to us through the poetical books of the Old Testament: "Or ever the silver cord be loosed, or the golden bowl be broken, or the pitcher be broken at the fountain, or the wheel broken at the cistern." What cord, what is it for? what bowl, whose pitcher? All silver cords, of course, all pitchers; the function of such language is always symbolic.

A dozen years after *The Waste Land*, Eliot permitted

himself in *The Rock* to narrow this mode of eloquence
into a catchy device:

> In the land of lobelias and tennis flannels
> The rabbit shall burrow and the thorn revisit,
> The nettle shall flourish on the gravel court.

As a poetic figure, concrete universals occupy a kind of
indistinct limbo between the more established symbolic
image such as Eliot's later rose garden, which may be said
to *contain*, by inheritance, *its own meaning*, and the
simpler, half-symbolic and half-illustrative concrete image,
of which Eliot made striking if perhaps showy use when
the Tempters in *Murder in the Cathedral* announce that

> All things are unreal,
> Unreal or disappointing:
> The Catherine wheel, the pantomime cat,
> The prizes given at the children's party,
> The prize awarded for the English Essay,
> The scholar's degree, the statesman's decoration.

When the universal side of the figure is left unlimited,
a great deal of resounding wind may pass itself off as
wisdom. In *The Waste Land*, however, the imagery and
the biblical parallelism that goes with it are not carried
on too long and are embedded in a more modest context
of the specific: the lines on "the dead tree" and "the cricket"
are restrained within bounds between the limits of "*this*
stony rubbish," which precedes them, and the shadow of
"*this* red rock," which follows. The opening of "What the
Thunder Said" is again made up of these universalized
images in parallel sequence, but again they are anchored
into the specific by their clear allusion to Christ in Gethse-
mane. In the final *Waste Land* this style remains under
control, in keeping with what it says, and is broken off
before it begins to mock itself, broken usually without
transition, by a contrasting passage. After the "handful
of dust," there enters, in the sailor's song from *Tristan*

und Isolde, the moment of hope in a new rhythm, new mood, even new language, and this in turn is followed by the willowy and fragile romantic moment of failed hope in the hyacinth garden. The whole sequence is then closed by the return to *Tristan*, this time the moment preceding death, conclusion of a failed hope; and, though in German, it answers also to Ezekiel, the cricket, the dry stone and the shadow, *"Oed' und leer das Meer,"* waste and empty the sea. After a longer pause Madame Sosostris enters, introduced by an offhand, colloquial town voice, to answer—but only with riddles from her Tarot cards which sum up the figures in the poem—the question that has been asked: Is there possible life in the stony rubbish?

The shifting of styles and voices between present and past forms part of the demonstration of "unity of culture," but thematically also, in the final form of the poem, the styles and voices fall into place, adjusted to each other throughout by often subtle means which render the discontinuities less abrupt and the disparate episodes less disparate than they appear. The two scenes representing sexual frustration in "A Game of Chess" are at opposite poles in style, yet the poetic language and traditional rhythms of the first are punctuated by humdrum reference to hot water and a closed car, and by a snatch of the "Shakespeherian Rag." [j] In the second, the gossip of Lil's

j Though it is incorrectly identified in David Ward's recent book on Eliot, many readers now know that "that Shakespeherian Rag" is not a made-up title. A popular song of 1912, the words of its chorus were reprinted by R. B. McElderry, Jr., in *American Quarterly* IX (1957). The quotation in *The Waste Land* is inexact: its prefatory "O"s and the extra syllable in "Shakespearian" are not in the song—cannot, in fact, be accommodated to its tune—and Eliot reversed the two following lines, somewhat inaccurately. Whether his memory slipped or whether he meant to rag the ragtime further is uncertain, but I should guess the former. In quoting for serious purposes, his verbal memory was not infallible (see, for example, his clearly unintentional misquotation of Shakespeare, noted here in Chapter 9); and I am inclined to think he may simply have confused one old tune with another. A better-known song of the same period (1910-20), "Oh, You Beautiful Doll," has been suggested to me by Russell

friend, spoken in the language of low life, proceeds under
the shadow of the recurring "HURRY UP PLEASE ITS TIME";
and at the end the gentle echoing voice of Ophelia's last
farewell, "Good night, sweet ladies, good night, good night,"
serves not only as the poet's ironic comment on the scene
but also, since it is the voice of the victim in *Hamlet*, serves
to mark an essential pathos beneath the coarse surface
of Lil's story. Even if we cannot be sure that the poet
himself was as vividly aware of the pathos as of the irony,
still the episode of Lil, thus dignified, is brought within
range of the distraught voices in the preceding "Cleopatra"
scene.

In her good night, Ophelia may just barely have edged
out Virginia Woolf. Eliot had recently read and admired
her new book of stories and sketches *Monday or Tuesday*,
and, as her diary reported the conversation, "he picked
out the String Quartet, especially the end of it," for his
chief praise. "The String Quartet" is made up of shifting
imagery running parallel to shifting themes and moods
of the music; it ends with a repeated farewell as the
musicale breaks up:

"Good night, good night. You go this way?"
"Alas. I go that."

The final line echoes in a key as solitary as Eliot's own
frail bridge of ivory chessmen, a mood (or if not a mood,

---

and Marcia Astley. Its concluding line is prefaced by four "Oh"s, and
the tune of this line fits Eliot's first line accurately with the doubled
syllable in "Shakespeherian" marking the metrical anticipation characteristic of ragtime's syncopation. The tune does not take care of Eliot's
other lines, however. Trivial though the question is, there is a real, if
minor, difference in tone between an inexactly remembered snatch of stale
popular song and a deliberate, pointless parody of it. (In addition to the
Astleys, Martin Silver, and Bill Lichtenwanger, I am indebted for this
still inconclusive note to the aid of Mr. and Mrs. Elmer Blende of Blende's
Mission Music, Santa Barbara.)

a theme) not altogether lost even through the vulgar transposition of Lil's story. "The eyes of others our prisons; their thoughts our cages. Air above, air below." Eliot read these words too from *Monday or Tuesday* (in "An Unwritten Novel"); and they may have had as much to do as Petronius or James with the original title "In the Cage" and its Heraclitean "air." [k]

The shadows in the whole of "A Game of Chess" are easily obscured by the prevailingly bright hard light of its surface, a flaw, it may be, in the writing and not only in our reading of it. The shadows, nevertheless, are present, and so are the links of these scenes to each other and to the whole of the poem. At the end, the prison of Coriolanus in "What the Thunder Said" is still the prison of the self, the unbreakable solitude, as Eliot's note to those lines, quoting F. H. Bradley, makes explicit.

In "The Fire Sermon," the contemporary episode of the typist, related in uncontemporary rhyme, is tied to antiquity through its ostensible narrator Tiresias and then, by transformation of verse forms in its final quatrain, is returned altogether to the present world.

[k] In discussing the poems of Eliot, I have tried to avoid reference to inessential sources, most of all tenuous ones; and this of Virginia Woolf is exceedingly tenuous, since Ophelia's words are unmistakably those of the poem. Yet I find it difficult to forget the appositeness of the solitary-sounding last words in the story or to forget Eliot's having singled them out just as *The Waste Land* was at last getting properly under way but before Part II, at least in its present form, existed. With fragile sanity all about—Virginia's, already acknowledged and half perceptible even in "The String Quartet," Vivien's, and his own not altogether steady balance at the time, the prose lines might have brought Ophelia's farewell to mind. Short of death, madness is the ultimate solitude. At least, Ophelia's words are to be read as more than an accident of verbal association, introduced after "Ta ta. Goonight" for shock value alone. See Virginia's diary of 7 June 1921, quoted in Quentin Bell's *Virginia Woolf* (London, Hogarth, 1973), II, 78n; and *Monday or Tuesday* (New York, Harcourt, 1921), pp. 80,58-59. These associations, together with the restored ivory men who "make company between us," reinforce throughout Part II deeper undertones of which I, for one, had in the past been imperfectly aware.

She turns and looks a moment in the glass,
Hardly aware of her departed lover;
Her brain allows one half-formed thought to pass:
'Well now that's done: and I'm glad it's over.'
When lovely woman stoops to folly and
Paces about her room again, alone,
She smoothes her hair with automatic hand,
And puts a record on the gramophone.

The almost staid Drydenesque or eighteenth-century quatrains of the narrative accelerate into Goldsmith's single
jaunty line ("When lovely woman stoops to folly"), which
immediately, by addition of an extra upbeat "and" at the
end, transforms Goldsmith into what we now see he
virtually was to begin with, the gramophone's ragtime,
which is the rhythm of the quatrain that closes the episode.
In what follows, ragtime-Goldsmith is metamorphosed into
music from *The Tempest* heard "along the Strand," and
Shakespeare is thus transformed into (Shakespeherian) rag
for the second time in the poem. Musical wit makes its
comment in this sequence.

There is no need to plod through all these intricacies
of structure; it is enough to have observed one or two and
thereafter to sense their presence in the texture of the
whole poem: they have much to do with our sense of a
forward movement propelling *The Waste Land* toward its
final ambiguous resolution. By comparison with this,
Gerontion, for all its interest, is a half-formed work the
intent of which was never quite crystallized within its
impressive frame. In *The Waste Land* the intent, the
prevailing tone, possibly even the theme itself may have
discovered themselves fully only as the poem developed
and particularly as the concluding section was reached.
That discovery seems to have been verified and reinforced
when Eliot and Pound got together on the final revision.
But the substance, including even such firm, subtle weav-
ings of outwardly incongruous materials as we see in many

sequences as they now stand, were all present earlier. *The Waste Land* is still often read as a harsh bright satire or series of satires and parodies; and much of it, certainly, is entertaining on this level alone. Beneath all the glitter, nevertheless, lies a poem, not necessarily a poem perfectly realized through every line, but certainly one that is more "intensely serious" than the preceding *Burbanks* and *Sweeneys* had been and one that as a whole succeeds in conveying its seriousness along with its glitter. [1]

[1] For an antidote, however, to our over-solemn acceptance of *The Waste Land* whole as the summit of both art and wisdom, as well as for other salutary warnings, we may do well to read or reread Ian Hamilton's eminently unillusioned short essay on the poem in *Eliot in Perspective: A Symposium*, ed. Graham Martin (London: Macmillan, 1970).

6

Drumbeats: Hollow Men
and the End of Sweeny

"What's that that whimpers over'ead?" said Files-on-Parade.

Three poems of the decade following *The Waste Land*, as different from each other as poems of Eliot can well be, are linked by technical exploration in a direction to which Arnold Bennett provides the key, if a key is needed. Two works, the *Sweeney Agonistes* fragment and *The Hollow Men*, date from approximately the same time, late 1924 (*The Hollow Men* continuing on into 1925); *Coriolan*, the third, came some six or seven years later. The key, at its simplest and in a word, is the rhythm of the drumbeat, which has, however, more complex origins than the term alone suggests, for Eliot's interest in it was more than momentary. Late in 1923 he had drawn the subject into his review of a book on the Fool in Elizabethan drama; to which he gave the title "The Beating of a Drum."[1] After saying briefly what he had to say about the book and the fool, he turned to the subject of rhythm, which he thought "so utterly absent from modern drama" yet which today was the making of such "great actors" as Massine and Charlie Chaplin. What he chiefly had to say followed:

> An unoccupied person, finding a drum, may be seized with a desire to beat it; but unless he is an imbecile he will be unable to continue beating it, and thereby satisfying a need (rather than a "desire"), without finding a reason for so doing. The reason may be the long continued drought. The next generation or the next civilization will find a more plausible reason for beating a drum. Shakespeare and Racine—or rather the developments which led up to them— each found his own reason. The reasons may be divided into tragedy and comedy. We still have similar reasons, but we have lost the drum.

Sweeney Agonistes was meant to repair the loss, quite literally.

SWEENEY AGONISTES

By the time he visited Bennett in the fall of 1924, Eliot had more or less clearly in mind a dramatic plan of his own, and the purpose of his visit was to seek advice. According to Bennett's *Journal,* Eliot now wished to write a "drama of modern life (furnished flat sort of people) in a rhythmic prose 'perhaps with certain things in it accentuated by drum-beats.' And he wanted my advice. We arranged that he should do the scenario and some sample pages of dialogue."[2]

Like Henry James before him, Eliot had been bitten by the desire to write for the stage. Since 1918 he had been reading, lecturing, and writing about the problems of Elizabethan and Jacobean drama, and as early as 1920 he had thought of "the music-hall comedian" as a possible starting place for a development of modern poetic drama. His recent essay (February 1924) on "Four Elizabethan Dramatists: A Preface to an Unwritten Book" throws light, as usual, on what he had in mind. The essay had been severe upon even the best of the old dramatists, including Shakespeare, for their failure to invent or revive some "convention" within which their work could be contained. An artist's material, he explained, is always "actual life"; nevertheless, "an abstraction from actual life is a necessary condition to the creation of the work of art," and a convention provides the frame for that abstraction. The convention may be old or new, may govern either the subject matter or the technique, may be "any form or rhythm imposed upon the world of action"; but it must be consistently maintained, like the formal convention within which classical ballet has its consistent being.[3] *Sweeney Agonistes* was meant to repair this too.

Though in writing *The Waste Land* Eliot had initially meant to "do the Police in different voices," in the end the only passages conspicuously answering to that intention were the scenes involving Madame Sosostris and Lil. Other voices vary in mood, tone, even style, but are not ventriloquy, scarcely even when Goldsmith is briefly parodied: Sweeney's night out having been canceled, all but those other two voices speak the language of the cultivated and the literary with no strong idiosyncrasy other than the author's. The real speech one uses in conversation, Eliot knew, has to be distilled in poetry, usually stripped, always in some degree stylized; and with the aid of John Davidson and Laforgue he had early mastered the stylization of such English as he himself might use in conversation. A more severe stylization, however, is required if for a sophisticated poetic end one means to speak the language of the unsophisticated or the man in the street, and though Eliot had a good ear for varieties of speech it had not been at first infallible. When Lil's friend speaks in *The Waste Land*, Eliot had groped for his opening: "When Lil's husband was coming back out of the Transport Corps" was tried, and "Discharged out of the army??." It was

Pound apparently—with an ear that *was* infallible when
he chose to listen to it instead of to the ghost of James
Whitcomb Riley—who found the inevitable word in World
War I slang for *demobilized*, "When Lil's husband got
demobbed, I said—." [a]

After *The Waste Land*, Eliot's main line of poetic
development was toward something very different from
this: it took a direction pointed by the poetically heightened "What the Thunder Said," toward a frankly poetic
style; but interest in the vernacular and the drumbeat
persisted long enough to influence the two extended fragments and *The Hollow Men. Sweeney Agonistes* nominally
marks the beginning of Eliot's career as a dramatist, but
among his plays it had no sequel. Eliot always published
it not as a play but under the heading of "Unfinished
Poems," where also it proved rather a dead end, related
more nearly to parts of the later fragment *Coriolan* than
to anything else that followed it.

In *The Waste Land*, the stylization of Lil's story had
been minimal, and its verse rhythm minimal also; it was
real vernacular talk tightened, and ringing faintly of blank
verse. What was now needed for *Sweeney* was rhythmic
energy, but a factitious, mechanical energy, which would
function as both an expression of the life of Dusty and
Doris and Sweeney and a commentary upon it. The opening
dialogue between Dusty and Doris is then an extreme
rhythmic formalization of the flat speech in which each
speaker parrots the other's two-beat mechanical half-line,
in a stylization of the vacuous as exact as if it were a
ballet. The drumbeat, the stamping and shuffling of feet,
the stylized gesture and speech of the English music hall
and probably also of American vaudeville and minstrel

[a] *WL Facs.*, p. [13]. It is one of the very few specific words provided
by Pound if it was indeed he. For a recent indication that it may have
been supplied by Vivien Eliot, see Helen Gardner's account in Litz, p.
77.

show, together with the patterned rhythms of the *Barrack Room Ballads*—these are what we hear, with strains of Gilbert and Sullivan occasionally breaking in:

DUSTY: How about Pereira?
DORIS: What about Pereira?
         I don't care.
DUSTY: You don't care!
         Who pays the rent?
DORIS: Yes he pays the rent
DUSTY: Well some men don't and some men do
         Some men don't and you know who
DORIS: You can have Pereira
DUSTY: What about Pereira?

And Dusty and Doris proceed to read their future in cards.

Out of this texture was to have been created not a simple satire on lower-class vacuity but a verse drama with serious symbolic meaning, a meaning of which one of the characters should be fully aware, as Eliot explained several years later. His intention had been

> to have one character whose sensibility and intelligence should be on the plane of the most sensitive and intelligent members of the audience; his speeches should be addressed to them as much as to the other personages in the play—or rather, should be addressed to the latter who were to be material, literal-minded and visionless, with the consciousness of being overheard by the former. There was to be an understanding between this protagonist and a small number of the audience, while the rest of the audience would share the responses of the other characters in the play.[4]

In the second of the two scenes drafted on this plan, Sweeney tells the story of a man who "did a girl in" and kept her in lysol in the bathtub; he announces that there is no reality except "Birth, and copulation, and death," and that "Life is death." And there is a knock upon the door, nine knocks, to be exact. As Doris's fortune card had been "the *two of spades*! THAT'S THE COFFIN!!," as she had exclaimed in alarm, it may be imagined that Sweeney will perhaps do her in. "Any man has to," he had said, "needs to, wants to/ Once in a lifetime, do a girl in."

No wonder the play was never finished. In the characters of Dusty and Doris and Sweeney—whether the Sweeney of earlier poems or a namesake—Eliot had scarcely given himself scope for a character of superior "sensitivity and intelligence" who would address the correspondingly superior few in the audience, while ostensibly merely entertaining the "visionless." Sweeney seems already too firmly fixed on a single level to be susceptible of transformation into that consciously symbolic truth-speaker. Doris, with her fortune-telling cards, might have functioned as an unconscious intuitive Madame Sosostris, but this would not have forwarded the design for a consciously perceptive protagonist.

Eliot once sketched a conclusion for the second Sweeney scene; but even though the sketch dates from the same months (early 1933) as his serious account of the subtle symbolism he had intended, what the sketch presents can hardly be taken with that degree of seriousness. In the continuation, the knocks at the door, of which nine occur at the end of the printed play, are doubled to eighteen, "like the angelus," Eliot wrote, and they usher in an "old gentleman" who is in evening dress but "otherwise resembles closely Father Christmas." His name, he announces, is Time; and he comes from "the vacant lot in front of the Grand Union Depot," where he waits "for the lost trains that bring in the last souls after midnight." He answers Sweeney's question, "When will the barn-fowl fly before morning?/ When will the owl be operated on for cataracts? . . ." in corresponding terms:

> "When the camel is too tired to walk farther
> Then shall the pigeon-pie blossom in the desert
> At the wedding-breakfast of life and death."

And Father Time departs, as "the alarum clock in his hand goes off."

For its presentation, Eliot explained, "the action should be stylised as in the Noh drama"; and he recommended that Pound's book on that subject and Yeats's directions for *The Hawk's Well* be consulted. The actors were to wear masks; "the whole play [was] to be accompanied by light drum taps to accentuate the beats (esp. the chorus, which ought to have a noise like a street drill)." [b]

The symbolism of either Sweeney or the old gentleman named Time would not much strain the dullest of wits; and though the letter providing this conclusion does not read as if Eliot were playing a practical joke on the girls at Vassar, the ending can scarcely be read as anything but a jocular burial of a hopelessly false start, which clearly had no future of the sort he had projected. The plan for this sort of double communication had to await *The Family Reunion*, which has Agatha for its more conceivable double-speaker of wisdom. The fragment of *Sweeney* which Eliot himself printed, however, does have limited success of a limited kind. The characters are all flat and none seems capable of development into anything else; but the poet succeeds in making his own comment all the same, for his irony pervades their speeches: their talk and their souls are filtered through the drumtap rhythm (which needs no reinforcement from actual drums to be heard) and the stylization. What Eliot in fact conveys by technical means is his own disgust, relieved by amusement, at the human world of Sweeneys and Dorises and Dusties.

[b] This conclusion and the instructions are contained in a letter to Hallie Flanagan, who was staging *Sweeney Agonistes* in her experimental theater at Vassar. She prints Eliot's letter with her account of the performance, which Eliot, in America for lectures, attended (*Dynamo*, New York: Duell, Sloan and Pearce, 1943, pp. 82-85). Whether or not Eliot expected that she would print his conclusion does not appear to be known.

THE HOLLOW MEN

> The eyes of others our prisons.
> (Virginia Woolf in *Monday or Tuesday*)

Meantime, *The Hollow Men*, which I. A. Richards once thought Eliot's "most beautiful" poem, was under way. First published as a whole in *Poems 1909-1925*, it is made up of parts, each of which except the last (along with two other lyrics that now appear among Eliot's "Minor Poems") had been published as separate poems at least twice during the preceding year.[5] Precisely when these were composed is uncertain, but *The Hollow Men* itself is a lyrical distillation of the spirit, once more, of a waste land, this time a land unrelieved by hope. There is no Grail and no Quest, no lands will be set in order, and the desolate inhabitants know their plight. [c] In mood, the poem is as clearly defined as any of Eliot's long poems; in details of conceptual meaning it is his most obscure, and not to its advantage.

The final line has gained the currency of a proverb: "Not with a bang but a whimper." The key word in the line is "whimper," and the prime inspirer of the word is Kipling.

> "What's that that whimpers over'ead?" said Files-on-Parade,
> "It's Danny's soul that's passin' now" the Colour-Sergeant
> said.

[c] Friedrich W. Strothmann and Lawrence V. Ryan, in "Hope for T. S. Eliot's 'Empty Men' " (*PMLA* LXXIII [1958], pp. 426-432), argue with a good deal of ingenuity a contrary view, that hope is the real point of the poem. That the men are "empty," they maintain, means that they are in a condition described by St. John of the Cross, of readiness for the mystic vision. In the "prickly pear" they find the symbol of Christ crowned with thorns, "the still point of the turning world" for the circling children. Skilfully presented though the argument is, the overwhelming spirit of the poem, as well as its relatively early date, seems to me to preclude such a reading. And as for the crown of thorns, I stick by the tradition of its being from the jujube-tree (Zizyphus spina Christi), or perhaps the species of euphorbia still known as "crown of thorns." Prickly pear cactus, in any event, does not readily bend itself, even symbolically, into a circlet or crown, as I imagine Eliot would have known.

Eliot expressly admired Kipling's use of the word *whimper*
and admired the whole of *Danny Deever* as "technically
remarkable" in its "combination of heavy beat and variation of pace"; it was what Eliot needed at the time,
drumbeats again, heavy, but now with variation of pace.
In the past, his rhythms when they were not altogether
regular had lain for the most part within the possible
bounds of blank verse as it appeared at its freest in the
late plays of Shakespeare and other Jacobean drama, with
the further freedom of certain poems of Arnold and Swinburne. He was ready for something else; and, as parts of
The Hollow Men show by its absence, the one thing needed
was energy.

Turning, in his discussion of Kipling, to "other poets"
(himself), Eliot spoke of the poem that begins "to shape
itself in fragments of musical rhythm" without conscious
thought of any meaning. But he warned that in the end
"the music of verse is inseparable from the meanings and
associations of words." [d] This is all very well. Eliot-as-Pos-
sum once characterized poetic meaning—in some kinds of
poetry, not all, he was careful to add even then—as "a
bit of nice meat" brought by the burglar for the house-dog.[6]
In my own experience with *The Hollow Men*, what the
house-dog is offered is the smell of meat only, which being
either too much or too little, serves to waken the dog and
keep him on the prowl. With the intellect awake and
unsatisfied, emotion, imagination, "pure" aesthetic pleasure in the music or mood are gnawed away. Eliot was
himself, I think, too intellectual a poet to succeed with
no more than the smell of meaning; and in "The Music
of Poetry" he remarks that he has never met "poetry of

[d] Introduction to *A Choice of Kipling's Verse*, reprinted in *On Poetry
and Poets*, pp. 264-294; see especially pp. 271, 277-279. Eliot may also
have remembered the vivid *whimper* of Yeats's early line: "Desolate winds
that beat the doors of Heaven, and beat/ The doors of Hell and blow
there many a whimpering ghost" (in *The Unappeaseable Host*).

great musical beauty which made no sense." [e]

As completed, however, *The Hollow Men* is probably Eliot's nearest approach to pure "mood music," the early *Rhapsody* alone excepted. Attempts to read it in detail as symbolism with conceptual equivalents for all the images have been generally unsatisfactory: they are apt to end, even the best of them, as exposition of the epigraphs, and of the sources and the meaning of the sources, in the hope that the sum of these will elucidate the poem. The poem does make numerous statements, of which some embody clear conceptual meanings and others sound as if they must be pointing to private conceptual meanings (a few that may be guessed at). The sense of the whole is clear also: "we are the hollow men" is explicit enough and covers it, "our" life is meaningless, and the despairing mood in which "we" feel our hollowness is unmistakable. It does not even seem necessary to ask whether Eliot's "we" is purely editorial, or whether it represents part of the modern world or the whole. But in the middle, especially in the third and fourth divisions, the poem falls apart.

Rhythmically, all the interior stanzas are limp; they nearly whimper themselves. And as they proceed, they increasingly suggest the writings of a poet in a despairing mood half-idly and without much energy exploring verbal patterns and patterns of images and half-thoughts, hoping that from this activity something will grow. As, in a limited way it does; but nothing quite vital grows, and these interior stanzas remain blurred by what seems a failure of adjustment between will and impulse at a time when the vitality of both will and impulse is low.

[e] *On Poetry and Poets*, p. 21. With Pound, he had approved in 1917 Pater's dictum that "for poetry to approach the condition of music . . . it is not necessary that poetry should be destitute of meaning" ("Ezra Pound: His Metric and Poetry," *To Criticize the Critic*, p. 170. And by 1948 he was saying, "I think that poetry is only poetry . . . so long as the subject matter is valued for its own sake" ("From Poe to Valéry," *ibid.*, p. 39).

"The music of verse is inseparable from the meanings and associations of words."—"We are the hollow men" is a drumbeat line, "Trembling with tenderness" is nerveless. The lines scan alike, and the first, even, is smoother from the absence of stopped consonants, provided we ignore context, meaning, syntax. But the first is assertion, unmodified, downright, and followed by others like it—"We are the stuffed men"; the second is syntactical contingency hanging from a rhetorical question too weak even to require an interrogation mark. The music is not only "inseparable" from the meaning but in these lines is created by it; and differentiation of mood, rhythm, and sense is clear.

But problems arise from the recurring "words and their associations"—"eyes," "death," "kingdom," "a fading star," and words having to do with drought—which dominate the poem. Of kingdoms there are death's "other" kingdom, death's dream kingdom, a twilight kingdom, death's twilight kingdom, lost kingdoms, and the Kingdom of God; these may be reduced, according to various readings, to two, or three, or five, variously defined. There are direct eyes, eyes one fears to meet, eyes that are sunlight and eyes that are stars, there is absence of eyes and presence of blind eyes. Most of the kingdoms belong to death but death is not everywhere the same death. I list these not in mockery but to indicate the perplexity of the house-dog, who will not go to sleep because he has had a sniff of meaning, because, in fact, the poem is enclosed within the very precise "meanings" of the drumbeat beginning and end. In between, however, the "meanings and associations" of the words become increasingly indeterminate, equations left insoluble by the presence of too many variables; and the result is not so much "suggestive" in the Symbolist sense as it is amorphous. As Eliot once said of Swinburne's words, "If they suggest nothing, it is because they suggest too much."[7]

Part of the difficulty, in addition to a general absence

of vitality, lies in a failure of adjustment of the parts to each other. Take, for example, the clear negative scarecrow image—part scarecrow and part Guy Fawkes effigy—of the opening and its half-positive appearance in Part II. It is the most noticeable instance because in itself Part II is the most nearly successful of the interior sections. Here, hollow, incapable of the right human response, and guilty by reason of being hollow, the speaker dreads encounter in dreams with accusing and self-accusing eyes. And so he dreams of escape into a deathlike kingdom that is not actual extinction but a half-existence in which there is no pain and no responsibility, for everything is beheld from far off. It is the realm of unhappy children's fantasies of suicide, or of Joyce's sick little boy imagining his own death with the satisfaction of being present at his own funeral to see his injury avenged. In that dream kingdom of the hollow man the dreaded eyes are transformed into benefi-cent "sunlight on a broken column"; the speaker need not try to be human, he is beyond blame and the eyes do not search him. Here, like stuffed rat or crow or scarecrow (clothes on "crossed staves"), oneself a stuffed magpie "alongside weasel and crow," he

> swings in the wind and rain,
> In the sun and in the snow,
> Without pleasure, without pain,
> On the dead oak tree bough.
> . . . .
> There are no more sins to be sinned
> On the dead oak tree bough.

I am quoting not *The Hollow Men* but Edward Thomas's *The Gallows*, which I think Eliot had in mind,[f] as well as the stuffed effigy, the now passive remains of that man

[f] Since 1917, Eliot had known the work of Thomas, whose *Collected Poems* first appeared in 1920. In 1936 its publication was taken over by Eliot's own firm, Faber and Faber.

of action Guy Fawkes. Eliot's hollow man wishes for the
shadowy existence of such "disguises":

> Rat's coat, crowskin, crossed staves
> In a field
> Behaving as the wind behaves
> No nearer—

Let this half-existence, he asks, preserve him from

>   that final meeting
> In the twilight kingdom
> [With eyes I dare not meet in dreams][8]

The real kingdom of death is not this dreamed escape,
as he knows, but a facing of truth, the kingdom that
Conrad's Kurtz recognized as "the horror," self-accusing
eyes of truth and guilt. Part II as a whole seems clear
and self-consistent: its dream of escape, first through
distance which removes the pain of life and so beautifies
it, then through "disguise" which protects the self from
its own or others' reproach. But, with respect to the whole
poem, all this leaves the very differently oriented feeling
of the opening hollow men in limbo. And in the parts that
follow till we reach the conclusion, the same problem arises,
intensified by absence of clarity in thought and feeling
within the parts as well as between them. The poet who
had created a poetic whole out of the most diverse material
in *The Waste Land* left the comparatively homogeneous
parts of *The Hollow Men* without focus.

The conclusion of the poem, however, comes clear again,
with the flaccid lyricism of the middle parts giving way
to a return of the drumbeat or the stamping of feet. The
reality is the cactus, not the rose (whether of love or of
religion, "the hope only of empty men"); Part V makes
it explicit. Between the parody of children's jingle-games
turned sterile as "we" circle the cactus of the desert instead
of the mulberry-bush in the garden—between this and its

sequel, three formulaic stanzas reiterate directly in abstract terms the essence of frustration: between all forms
of thought or wish or impulse and their fulfillment "falls
the Shadow," which from the tone of the whole we feel
as the failure of energy and will. "For thine is the Kingdom"
fails of completion, dwindling out of psychic weariness to
"For thine is   "; even the already tired affirmation that
"Life is very long" trails off in "Life is   "; till at length
we are caught up in the dead factitious energy of movement
in the final lines:

> *This is the way the world ends*
> *This is the way the world ends*
> *This is the way the world ends*
> *Not with a bang but a whimper.*

The echoes recalling defeated men of action—Guy
Fawkes, Mr. Kurtz ("he dead"), and Brutus die away too:
from the words of Shakespeare's troubled Brutus—

> Between the acting of a dreadful thing
> And the first motion, all the interim is
> Like a phantasma or a hideous dream
> > [II. i. 63-65. Brutus also speaks of "hollow men"
> > in IV. ll. 23]

—from this comes the formulaic center of Eliot's conclusion:

> Between the idea
> And the reality
> Between the motion
> And the act
> Falls the Shadow.

The waste land of the hollow men at the end is thus
translated into failure of will and energy; yet the hovering
presence of Kurtz, Guy Fawkes, and Brutus introduces
something equivocal that blurs the symbolism, for we

remember those, the "lost/ Violent souls," as men whose failures were failures of success, not of will (Brutus is a partial exception) and also as men whose will to act and whose actions had been better *un*conceived.

More than any other of Eliot's composite works, *The Hollow Men* seems to me to show its seams. I cannot escape the impression of its having been put together primarily out of thrift, as an ingenious means of preserving and making something out of short lyrics which never quite crystallized as lyrics and yet were too attractive to discard entirely. Many of us probably felt this before we knew the history of the publication of its parts. None of these needs its neighbor, and all the interior parts, though each does in fact say something different from the other, still sound repetitive, as if they have originated in separate repeated efforts to produce an effect that never quite defined itself. Their rhythm and style resemble the lyrical short-line passages in *The Waste Land* though their tone is more frankly personal, their rhythm a great deal more languid and lifeless; in spite of some fine and other fine-sounding lines, they are examples even more than they are expressions, of limpness.[g] To a degree Eliot saves them by framing them within the marked beats of the opening and the close. These beats—"We are the hollow men,"

[g] Part of the weakness of certain passages derives, one feels sure, from the inclusion of private matter which could not properly be made clear but which also had not been satisfactorily objectified. The theme of human love, for example, is introduced only to be dropped:

At the hour when we are
Trembling with tenderness
Lips that would kiss
Form prayers to broken stone.

The reader wishing to carry speculation further may consult the closing words of *The Use of Poetry*; his own knowledge of the life of Coleridge, to which Eliot's passage refers; Frank Morley's recollections of Eliot in Tate (pp. 104-105); and James Thomson's poem *Art*, Part III. The pursuit will answer no riddles in *The Hollow Men*, however.

"Shape without form," and "Here we go round the prickly pear," the last inseparable in the mind from its emphatic ritual of stamping and movement—provide what is, at any rate for hollow men, an appropriately factitious galvanized energy.

"Poetry begins," Eliot was to say a few years later, "with a savage beating a drum in a jungle," and he had already postulated this vital rhythm as the true origin of tragedy and comedy.[9] In his own hands the drum becomes something quite different: the dead drum of hollow men and the mechanical drumbeats of Dusty and Doris. This was what in the years between *The Waste Land* and *Ash Wednesday* he himself had to express. [h]

h It has been thought that much of the poem consists of material discarded by Pound or Eliot himself from *The Waste Land*. None of the parts appear in the surviving typescript (for one slight and indirect connection, see *WL Facs.*, pp. [99] and note, p. 129), but their presence at an earlier stage is not impossible. The complex publishing history of the separate parts and of the two other lyrics associated with them has defeated most critics but is correctly given in Gallup. The first group had appeared under the title "Doris's Dream Songs," suggesting a possible connection with *Sweeney Agonistes*; the title of the second group was noncommittal, "Three Poems"; the third introduced the present title and the Guy Fawkes epigraph. For details the reader should consult Gallup.

Ash Wednesday:
The Time of Change

> For now at this time is the turning of the year.... The
> creatures, the fowls of the air, the swallow and the turtle,
> and the crane and the stork, "know their seasons," and
> make their just return at this time every year. Every thing
> now turning, that we also would make it our time to turn
> to God in.
>
> Lancelot Andrewes, Sermon
> for Ash Wednesday, 1619.

An interval of some two years separates publication of *The
Hollow Men* from the earliest lyric of *Ash Wednesday*;
and during that interval the most highly publicized event
in the life of Eliot took place. Public though the outcome
was, however, no presently available records chronicle fully
the step-by-step development that led in 1927 to Eliot's
baptism and admission into the Church of England. His
prose tells us something, *Ash Wednesday* and the Ariel
poems something, each enough to shed limited light on
the other. Whatever the process, the change resulted in
a group of new and very different poems. Though the

conversion from his earlier scepticism undoubtedly had in some degree an emotional origin, as such changes normally have, the man known through either the poetry or the prose as the earlier Eliot does not suggest a temperament longing to throw itself into a whole-hearted devotion or even, quite, longing for a safe haven. Such evidence as we have points first to an intellectual rather than a directly emotional change. In 1932 Eliot said he thought "one of the reasons" for his conversion had been the conviction that the Christian scheme was "the only one which would work . . . . the only possible scheme which found a place for values which I must maintain or perish . . . , the belief, for instance, in holy living and holy dying, in sanctity, chastity, humility, austerity."[1] This was said in retrospect.

Earlier evidence suggests that he had been led first through mainly intellectual channels of influence from the thought of Irving Babbitt, T. E. Hulme, Charles Maurras, and others—with no little help also from certain aspects of his own temperament—to the Augustinian, anti-Rousseauist conviction of the sinful nature of man. This had been a major teaching of Babbitt in his attacks upon Rousseau and the Rousseauist aspects (which were all he saw) of Romanticism. *Rousseau and Romanticism* had appeared in the spring of 1919, but Eliot had come under the influence of Babbitt's thought much earlier as his student at Harvard and an admiring reader of his work. Babbitt's disapproval of the direction of American society, his iconoclasm and arrogance, his emphasis on discipline, doctrine, aristocratic values, and not least his hostility to Romanticism had from the beginning appealed to Eliot and influenced his views. Babbitt, however, held that man's imperfect nature might be controlled without doctrinaire religion by a "new Humanism," through development of what is commonly called conscience and what he called an "inner check." The conception is essentially—to oversimplify in summary—a development from Arnold's ideal of culture through which the Christian ethic and classic grace and "light" might be preserved and indeed strengthened, without the outworn aspects of Christian dogma. The voice of the Thunder in *The Waste Land*, "DA," is at home within this frame of thought. By 1927, however, Eliot had concluded that it would not do; and his essay of 1928 on "The Humanism of Irving Babbitt" attacks that position— attacks, that is, reliance upon any "inner check" not grounded in religious authority—and in the process records, partly by implication, a significant stage of his own thought, though this had been glanced at the year before in a review of F. H. Bradley.

In the following year (1929) he directed "Second Thoughts about Humanism," a much sharper attack—indeed for Eliot an exceptionally ill-natured piece of writing, exhibiting none of his earlier urbanity—this time against Norman Foerster, from whom he quotes a paragraph only to characterize it as "a composition of ignorance, prejudice, confused thinking and bad writing," adding presently with rather a sneer, "And if he [Foerster] thinks that religion depreciates science and art, I can only suppose that his religious training took place in the mountains of Tennessee." Memory of the Scopes trial was still fresh. Eliot's own position now followed that of T. E. Hulme, whose general view was that nothing short of dogmatic religion could serve to control man's evil nature; and in this essay Eliot quoted a passage from *Speculations* in which Hulme had stressed the importance for Christianity of the dogma of Original Sin and had concluded, "It is not, then, that I put up with the dogma for the sake of the sentiment, but that I may possibly swallow the sentiment for the sake of the dogma." Quoting this with evident approval, Eliot concluded his second attack on humanism: "Rational assent may arrive late [he himself was forty-one that year], intellectual conviction may come slowly, but they come inevitably without violence to honesty and nature. *To put the sentiments in order is a later, and an immensely difficult task*: intellectual freedom is earlier and easier than complete spiritual freedom" (my italics).[2]

On Eliot's invitation, humanism, Babbitt, the human will, the need for an "absolute" and "authoritative" church, and the value of increasing rather than reducing the power of the Church within the State were much debated in *Criterion* during these years, by others as well as himself, though as editor he was scrupulous in affording space to opposing views; even Foerster had his say at length, and the debate spilled over further into political and literary articles written from various angles. But Eliot's own position was made clear in *Criterion* as well as elsewhere, in repeated sharp attacks upon his old friend Bertrand Russell (to whom as mathematician he usually first made a polite but perfunctory bow) and milder ones on the humanism of Ramon Fernandez, in signed reviews of books on religion, in certain of the essays collected in *For Lancelot Andrewes* (1928). Though the ideal of unity of culture, which had prevailed a few years earlier, still underlies much of the writing, it is often well buried under authoritarian views on Church and State.

The tone of Eliot's prose during these years has the certitude of Papal pronouncements, though from time to time he protests his ignorance *pro forma* ("I know nothing whatever of economics, but. . . ."—a trick of arrogance he may have picked up from F. H. Bradley, whose "habit of discomfiting an opponent with a sudden profession of ignorance" he had noticed in his essay of 1927). In nearly all this polemical writing emphasis is laid upon the institutional—Church, State, Monarchy—and the philosophical-dogmatic, with rarely a word about the individual soul, his own or others'. It was the period of his celebrated announcement, issued in the manner of a public proclamation, that his position was now "classicist in literature, royalist in politics, and anglo-catholic in religion." [a] Reading through these and other writings of the period, one finds Eliot becoming convinced, like Hulme, that society needs orthodox Christianity for moral and civilizing reasons; there is at first no indication that he himself is in any real sense a believer: "Few people are sufficiently civilized to afford atheism," he remarked in passing, as late as 1928.[3] Such a position, however, is ultimately untenable for a man of conscience who aspires to honesty and for one with Eliot's awareness of his own strain of arrogance: if others need religion to make them decent human beings, who am I to think myself an exception? The imperative that this leads to is clear, one must *will* oneself into religious belief; and we are hereupon returned to the question of change in the inner man, in oneself not others, and to change that is not intellectual only. We are also returned from the prose back to the poetry. Studded though it is with clues to the poetry and occasional clues even to his private experience, the prose of Eliot is always prose of the public platform; there is no intimacy in it. Neither is there much intimacy, if we look back, in the earlier poetry, not much express intimacy, that is, in spite of its many personal elements. Dating from the time of his formal admission into the Church, however, a new and frankly personal tone enters into Eliot's poetry, and with the new tone comes once more a new style.

Indissoluble in the final effect of these poems, the new tone and style cannot be characterized together or in similar terms, for the key to one is intimacy, to the other what would seem its opposite, ritual. *Ash Wednesday* is confessional; and through other poems of this period, in

[a] Preface to *For Lancelot Andrewes* (1928). Eliot later regretted its manner, if not its substance. Babbitt, he said, when the two met in London had reproached him for not making his changed convictions public, and this had led to his unnecessarily proclamatory statement.

spite of expressly named dramatic personae, the poet's personal voice is heard and clearly meant to be heard with a directness that is new. Yet the style is less markedly individual, less idiosyncratic than before; it is in fact impersonal, deriving largely from the language and rhythm of church ritual and the poetical books of the King James Bible, a language universal in its associations, for the most part lofty, and highly poetical in the traditional sense of that term. Though *The Waste Land* had contained important passages of Old Testament "poetical" poetry (notably the "son of man" passage in Part I and the opening of Part V), as well as other frankly poetical passages, in general Eliot's style in verse down to the time of his conversion had remained deliberately anti-poetical; afterwards, except for certain passages in the *Four Quartets*, it rarely descends from the "high" poetical, still, however, retaining some of the living sinew of speaking inflections. It is in this new style that *Ash Wednesday* and the Ariel poems come to explore the inner reality of a changed and changing self.

In its final form *Ash Wednesday* is one poem, and I wish to speak of it as a poetic whole, but as it was not at first a whole, something is also to be said of its parts. The first three appeared originally as separate poems published a year apart, the second appearing first, in 1927, under the title "Salutation"—the new Christian presumably saluting the world. The Poundian aura makes its title a trifle wry, but there is nothing either wry or Poundian in the poem itself. Still, the tone is not quite throughout the tone of the later Eliot: there is even a hint of something jaunty about it, as if the poet were faintly embarrassed by his new role though determined to carry it through.

> Lady, three white leopards sat under a juniper-tree
> In the cool of the day, having fed to satiety
> On my legs my heart my liver and that which had been
>   contained

> In the hollow round of my skull. And God said
> Shall these bones live? . . .

The grotesque imagery here rather takes the edge off the seriousness, as if the speaker hesitated to commit himself entirely; and the movement of the verse, neither quite metrical nor at all prosaic, is oddly light. So the verse and tone, but the substance is fully serious: it represents a negative stage in the progress of the Christian soul, the dissolution of the old self that has been held together by individual will and desire. The bones in the desert, dismembered remains of the old self, speak accepting their dismemberment, and the acceptance now enables them to sing their lyric hymn to the Virgin. Thus the Rose garden may flower in the desert.

The apparent immediacy of this poem (Part II, that is, of the final work), unlike the rest of *Ash Wednesday*, is essentially unreal, is indeed purely nominal. Though the bones speak directly of themselves in the first person, "I" and "we," in the language of Ezekiel and Isaiah, and of Elijah sitting under a juniper tree ("I who am here dissembled/ Proffer my deeds to oblivion," and "We are glad to be scattered . . ./ with the blessing of sand,/ Forgetting themselves and each other, united/ In the quiet of the desert")[b] and although the corresponding passage in Ezekiel is used in liturgy to represent the regeneration of baptism and the poem belongs to the year of Eliot's own baptism—in spite of this and much else that is nominally personal, the actual tone is not so. The lines, moreover, assert more than is felt to be quite true, as if the speaker were seeing a distant though vivid and hallucinatory vision of the dissolution of the old willful self rather than ex-

---

[b] See Ezekiel 37: "the valley which was full of bones." The whole chapter should be reread. For the rose in the desert, see Isaiah 35:1-2; and perhaps for the image of the devouring beasts, Jeremiah 5:5-6 as well as Dante's much-disputed Leopard, Lion, and She-Wolf in *Inferno* I:32-60.

periencing it. The directly physical legs, liver, skull, the "three leopards," the bones, the address to the mysterious "Lady," all have an extraordinary brightness but also a visionary quality, the remoteness of which is not due merely to the fact that they are symbolic. It is partly a result of the grotesquerie but even more a result of brightness and stillness: no conflict is implied, no effort, no strain, no hint that the self has experienced any difficulty in dissolving his will; and for this reason instead of being through-and-through grotesque the effect is one of a distant half-real serenity.

The opening images—"Lady," the precise pictorial "three white leopards," the biblical "cool of the day"—cancel all that should otherwise be painful, even the remnants of "legs," "heart," "liver," "brain": there is no gore, there has not been any gore. The Lady is immaculate, in white, the leopards are white, unsmudged by their feast, the bones are already by evening dry and shining. It is a still picture, creating even out of what should be movement between past and future a kind of stillness:

> And I who am here dissembled
> Proffer my deeds to oblivion, and my love
> To the posterity of the desert and the fruit of the gourd.

This is a ritual that has been enacted; it is not a direct experience. I read the disputed word *dissembled* in its rare and old sense of "disassembled," with perhaps an additional secondary implication not inconsistent with this, in the usual sense of the word, "disguised," like the hollow men in rat's coat, crowskin—essential anonymity. There is stillness or repose too in the song the bones sing to the Virgin, for it is all praise and no asking. The peace is in contrast to nearly all the rest of *Ash Wednesday* in which there is effort and little serenity, and in which all the prayers are pleas.

The place of this desert-and-rose-garden scene in the

final poem is somewhat ambiguous, for in Christian thought that influenced Eliot, notably that of St. John of the Cross, this dissolution of the individual will is an early stage after repentance; in *Ash Wednesday* it quite logically precedes the stage of toiling up the stairs. Its unreality remains so strongly felt in the context of the whole poem, however, that it may best be read as an as-if, a vision, at this stage, of the peace which the speaker of the preceding section imagines but does not quite experience as reality; having had even a vision of that willess state, however, he is enabled to struggle on. Subsequently he confesses the imcompleteness of his "turning."

Part I, though a year after "Salutation" it too appeared as a separate poem, sets in motion the larger final work. Its tone and not, as in Part II, its pronouns only, is personal, removed from immediacy only by the liturgical language and rhythms and only so far as is needed for the aesthetic decency of poetry. It also provides the formula for enclosure of the final poem, setting off a single cycle of change: "Because I do not hope to turn again," presently reinforced —"Because I *cannot* hope"—which becomes in the conclusion "*Although* I do not hope . . .": an essential turning accomplished, but a turn barely perceptible and barely more than a beginning.

The original title of Part I when it appeared alone, "Perch' io non spero" connects the poem explicitly with the opening of the poem of Cavalcanti written in exile to his Lady, "Perch' io non spero di tornar giammai"; but the figure of turning and turning again also, more significantly, leads back to Lancelot Andrewes's sermon for Ash Wednesday on the text "Therefore also now, saith the Lord, Turn ye even to Me . . . ," a sermon in which every possible visual and verbal variation is played on the word *turn*.

The experience of conversion presented by Eliot is poles distant from the easy evangelism of "come to Jesus and he will take away your troubles"; Eliot's Christianity belongs to the very different tradition of a long, narrow, difficult but necessary way, in which there may be more pain than joy, and very little ease. In this form of Christian thought the will plays a double role. For the individual will must be dissolved through identification with the will of God: "Teach us to care and not to care" is Eliot's formulation of this. It is what the poet prays for at the beginning of *Ash Wednesday* and what he is still only praying for at the end, where its meaning is placed beyond dispute by the addition of Dante's words "Our peace in His will." In absolute Christian terms no human will, however devout the Christian, is ever completely dissolved, and so all need to pray; but, as the context shows, Eliot means more than that: even in relative terms his humility has far to go. It is the individual will also, however, that, cooperating with supernatural grace, must will itself out of existence. Thus, in the opening part of *Ash Wednesday* the old self, out of despair and not the noblest kind of despair, undertakes to change by pure force of will. The mood is one which could find words through a line from the familiar, consciously paranoid sonnet of Shakespeare:

> Because I do not hope to turn
> Desiring this man's gift and that man's scope
> I no longer strive to strive towards such things
> (Why should the agèd eagle stretch its wings?)
> Why should I mourn
> The vanished power of the usual reign?
> . . . .
> Because I cannot hope to turn again
> Consequently I rejoice, having to construct something
> Upon which to rejoice.

Though despair, Eliot explains elsewhere, is "a necessary prelude to, and element in, the joy of faith,"[c] what the

---

[c] This statement concludes a significant passage in "The 'Pensées' of Pascal," 1931 (*Selected Essays*, p. 412). Much in that essay throws light on Eliot's own experience as an intellectual convert.

opening of *Ash Wednesday* presents does not in fact resemble that "blessed" and fruitful despair of St. John of the Cross; it is a more ordinary condition grounded in a sense of failure which seems only half sincere, a sense of frustration in the world's world. It is real enough itself, but the rejoicing that one still has to construct is more paradox than experienced joy and will not give the agèd eagle new wings. [d] It may lead the speaker to that distant vision of peace and gladness in the dismembered self of the scattered bones but not to the real experience of such a state.

The spiritual struggle of *Ash Wednesday* has its center in Part III, which in the order of composition followed Part I. When published alone in 1929, its title was "Al som de l'escalina," from which we know that we are to think of the *Purgatorio*: for the title is from a passage already drawn to our attention in Eliot's notes to *The Waste Land*: "Now I pray you, by that Goodness which guideth you to the summit of the stairway, be mindful" ['sovegna vos'—these words appear in the next section of *Ash Wednesday*] in due time of my pain." Visually the scene is the stair of a dark mediaeval tower up which the climber toils, at each turn leaving part of himself, or his former self, behind still "struggling with the devil of the stairs who wears/ The deceitful face of hope and of despair"—perhaps specifically the "demon of doubt" which, in the essay on Pascal, Eliot would soon describe as "inseparable from the spirit of belief." As this is surely

[d] The eagle of the opening lines suggests the agèd eagle of the mediaeval bestiary in which, representing the sinful soul, it falls into water and is renewed (a symbol of baptism); but there is so much of Dante in the whole of *Ash Wednesday* that the figure seems also ironically reminiscent of the eagles of the *Inferno* (Canto IV), the unbaptized great poets of antiquity—Homer and the rest, "those lords of highest song, which, like an eagle, soars above the rest"; these form a minor antithesis to the heavenly eagle of the *Paradiso*, of which Eliot speaks in his essay on Dante.

not true of all Christians, it may be supposed that he spoke
from his own as well as Pascal's experience of doubt. At
the landing of the third stair, looking out, he sees at a
distance the sensual world, focused in the broadbacked
Pan-like figure who reappears as "the garden god" in the
following section, a world of beauty and romance—of
hawthorn blossom, lilac, and a girl's brown hair "blown
over the mouth"—but he sees it only through the narrow
slotted window of the tower and climbs on through the
strength of pure will alone, the "strength beyond hope and
despair." This division of the poem concludes with what
I take to be a solemn pun embodying a confession.

In his prose, Eliot could be doctrinaire, illiberal, conde-
scending; he displayed no hesitations and few self-doubts.
He was under no obligation to make public confession of
his flaws, and he gave few hints of there being any. For
some years, indeed, beginning with his initial attacks on
humanism, his prose was often colored by a repellent
intellectual and moral-sounding arrogance. Prose, however,
one writes for the world, poetry largely for oneself; and
in his poetry Eliot subjected himself to a more rigorous
and self-critical criterion of sincerity than he seems to have
done in his prose.[e] Hence, as *Ash Wednesday* moves
toward the final reversal of the opening "Because I do
not hope," which will complete the change, acknowl-
edgments that the change will not be complete, or quite
pure, begin to appear. Yet now the tone of the poetry itself
does become more pure; the hint, which possibly I only
imagine I feel, of posturing in Parts I and II, disappears.
Part III concludes:

---

e Eliot's own well-known version of the difference—the "apparent
incoherence between my verse and my critical prose"—was that "in one's
prose reflexions one may be legitimately occupied with ideals, whereas
in the writing of verse one can only deal with actuality" (*After Strange
Gods*, p. 28).

Lord, I am not worthy
Lord, I am not worthy
                    but speak the word only.

In the account of the miracle in the gospel, the centurion
says to Christ: "Lord, I am not worthy that thou shouldest
come under my roof: but speak the word only, and my
servant shall be healed" (Matt. 8:5-8; cf. Luke 7:1-7). *Speak*
is grammatically in the second person, a petition; and Eliot
is using it no doubt in this sense, asking, though unworthy,
Christ's help. But I cannot escape from the other meaning
also, which the words bear as they stand, laid open by
the period and by omission of the centurion's concluding
words: Lord I am not worthy but *speak* the word only—that
is, I only speak it, I do not (or not yet) truly believe it.
The passage then is at once an affirmation and a denial
of the centurion's humility and faith, and constitutes a
preliminary half-offered confession of what is said explicitly
afterwards. It marks the progress, not so much in theme
as in tone, of the poet's peeling off of insincerities that
have been faintly perceptible even within this poem, in
the agèd eagle and the scattered bones.

Part IV returns to the desert and garden imagery of
Part II, but with the desert now remaining only as a
memory in the garden. Though the scene is more pageant-
like and processional than that of Part II, and though
there is no "I" or "we" to make it personal, and though
the Lady, supposing her to be the same lady, has been
rendered even more symbolic by the indeterminate pronoun and the tapestry-like flowers—"Who walked between
the violet and the violet"—still the mood is somehow
realized and experienced, not visionary or even distantly
beheld; the unmentioned speaker is in it, not imagining
it from elsewhere.

This is the scene of the poem (three of the sections are
"scenes" in the technical sense, the other three are meditations) that most nearly approaches the mood of beatitude;

there is repose and no struggle. Yet it has not the stillness, the motionless picture quality of Part II; it is all movement, a circumstance that may contribute to its greater reality and immediacy:

> Who walked between the violet and the violet
> Who walked between
> . . . .
> Going in white and blue, . . .
> . . . .
> Who moved among the others as they walked,
> . . . .
> Here are the years that walk between, bearing
> Away the fiddles and the flutes, restoring
> One who moves . . .
> . . . .
> The new years walk, restoring

This is a kind of royal progress, a formal procession. But through the symbolism, as the figure of the Lady, the veiled "Who," becomes presently "the years" and finally "the new years," real transformation is wrought in the subjective self. The sensual is purified: Pan's flute no longer is heard, and the chaste unicorns pass, drawing away the hearse of the outlived self with its once gilded youthful hopes, as the poet dedicates himself to his unknown future, "the unread vision in the higher dream."[f] The desert has become garden, the soul is restored and with it the creative

---

[f] Grover Smith (p. 319, n. 30) provides the source and hence the clue to the tantalizing mystery of the unicorns and the hearse (his interpretation of them, which however seems to me to miss the point, is on p. 151). They are not, as might have been supposed, something out of an old tapestry or mediaeval legend but an echo from Conrad Aiken's poem *Senlin: A Biography*:

> White unicorns come gravely down to the water.
> In the lilac dusk they come, they are white and stately.

Each stanza in Part 3 of Senlin's "Dark Origins" brings back these unicorns; and immediately following this, Part 4 is similarly dominated

spirit in a new vein, "restoring/ With a new verse the ancient rhyme." And so the effect of this procession, the last "scene" in the poem, is a remarkable combination of the inner and the outer world, processional yet experienced as spiritual reality. The poem does not end in beatitude, however, and this scene does not suggest that the end is won: it repeats the hortatory "redeem the time" and "redeem the dream"; the "word" is not yet quite "the Word," it is not yet quite heard or spoken, and so the soul is still in exile, but with hope, for he has had his moment in the garden.

The last two parts of *Ash Wednesday* are again, like the opening, meditations and not scenes. The scene of the fourth has led without a break into the quite extraordinary syntactical whirling about of *word* and *world* and *whirl* and *Word* that opens Part V. The syntax of this passage can be unwound, but I am not sure that it remains unwound; I find myself on most readings having to think it consciously all over again; and in any case, it seems to me too mannered to be poetically successful even with the precedent behind it of the Gospel of St. John and Lancelot Andrewes.[4] Its substance, however, is essential to the poem: it is an assertion of the truth of Christ as the Word, an assertion that this is the Reality even if one

---

by "white horses drawing a small white hearse." Senlin

> Regards the hearse with an introspective eye.
> "Is it my childhood there," he asks,
> "Sealed in a hearse and hurrying by?"

Finally, within the hearse, in the inmost of a series of coffins each within the preceding one, lies a "Princess! Secret of life!" who has "gilded mask, and jewelled eyes" (Aiken, *Collected Poems*, New York: Oxford, 1970, pp. 197-202). Both the imagery itself and what it symbolizes of dead youth and youth's impossibly jewelled and gilded hopes appear to be the materials which Eliot condensed for the conclusion of his pageant, marking a stage beyond the initial renunciation of past hope "because I do not hope to know again/ The infirm glory. . . ." The passage is Aiken Dantified, its obscurity sheltered under the authority of Dante's celebrated puzzles.

has not brought oneself to acknowledge it fully. The statements are made in general terms, but the whole has the tone of determined personal honesty as the poet goes on to describe the state of those who have espoused Christianity officially without their souls being fully committed. The indirect confession is reiterated some half-dozen times or more. First it is merely "those who walk among noise and deny the voice"; then the contradiction becomes more specific: will the sister "pray for/ Those who walk in darkness, who chose thee and oppose thee"; for "children at the gate/ Who will not go away and cannot pray" (like Herbert's "I could not go away, nor persevere," in *Affliction I*); "Pray for those who chose and oppose." Christ's reproach, which occurs in the ritual for Good Friday, is uttered twice: "O my people, what have I done unto thee." At last, in the most nearly self-damning words, "pray for those who . . . affirm before the world and deny between the rocks." Before the world Eliot had been "affirming" sometimes loudly in his prose, mainly by attacking scepticism, liberalism, and secularism in others; these words make clear that in the poem he is not merely describing the Christian's inevitable human imperfection in living up to his religion; he is deliberately confessing that his own public avowals are not or not yet entirely matched by private conviction.[g] This denial of belief, however, takes place "in the last desert between the last blue rocks/ The desert in the garden the garden in the desert"; hence, the direction is at least forward—"fare forward" was a phrase he came to love—and the red rocks of the waste land have become blue rocks, of "Mary's colour."

[g] The few statements having to do with doubt that I remember seeing in Eliot's prose appear deliberately ambiguous or, if one is unsympathetic, even sophistical; e.g., "doubt and uncertainty are merely a variety of Belief" ("A Note on Poetry and Belief," *The Enemy*, January 1927, p. 16); and see the statement on doubt and belief quoted earlier here from the essay on Pascal.

The following sixth and final section marks the change since the beginning: a change that is real but a good deal less than the poet has seemed publicly to claim for it—that was the burden of Part V; the new turning has been made by the will but not yet by the whole self. "Although" he does not hope or even quite wish to turn back to the old life, still he is filled with nostalgia. And since he is no longer shut up in his dark tower of intense struggle, the narrow "slotted window" through which he had seen the hawthorn and maytime and Pan is replaced now by a "wide window towards the granite shore" of the loved Massachusetts coast of his youth:

> And the lost heart stiffens and rejoices
> In the lost lilac and the lost sea voices
> And the weak spirit quickens to rebel
> For the bent golden-rod and the lost sea smell

(*bent* an extraordinarily vivid and economical epithet for the flower form of the finest of the goldenrods)

> The white sails still fly seaward, seaward flying
> Unbroken wings

—memories of the past in the sails and gulls and the eagle not yet agèd. The poet recovers briefly the very smell of the salt air, and the "blind eye" of memory revives the illusive hopes of the past—the "ivory gates" of the false dreams once harbored: nostalgia, all of it, for the dead hopes of the old self already borne away in the gilded hearse. This lost world of the senses is revived, enriched by the emotional freight of memory: the passage has a power new for Eliot, measurable by its distance from the vicarious nostalgia of the earlier "smell of hyacinths" in spring that recalled to him only the past desires of "other people." But broadbacked Pan is gone, along with the "brown hair" that distracted the climber of the stairs; and perhaps for this reason, perhaps also because it is all felt as "lost" and no longer hoped for, it is a memory that may be indulged freely without guilt through the "wide" window. Its spirit—"spirit of the river," the Mississippi of his childhood, "spirit of the sea"—even becomes part of the new life at the end of the poem as he invokes the "blessed sister" and "holy mother."

The whole of life is this mixed thing, a "dreamcrossed twilight between birth and dying" and

> the time of tension between dying and birth
> The place of solitude where three dreams cross.

The "three" may be the two he had recently described as the "high dream" of Dante and the Revelation of St. John and the "low dream" which is all that "the modern world seems capable" of, with the addition of one between, those lost dreams and aspirations of the old youthful life of reverie when one longed for the impossible, the "empty forms between the ivory gates."[h] It *is* a new life the poet has reached, yet the substance of his prayer is what it was at the beginning: "Teach us to care and not to care. ... Our peace in His will," preceded by a significant plea for sincerity. In the light of the dogmatic and sometimes arrogant assertions he was concurrently making in prose, this prayer must be seen as more than perfunctory: "Suffer us not to mock ourselves with falsehood." *Ash Wednesday*, then, though its theme is appropriate enough for the day that marks the beginning of Lent, is not merely the self-examination and repentance prescribed for the occa-

h I am not all certain of this reading of the "three dreams." If there were only two, they would seem obviously to be those he had described in his essay on Dante the year before (*Selected Essays*, p. 262), the "high" and the "low" that I refer to. Various other explanations have been offered by other writers for the "three": they include *past, present,* and *future*; the Lady, the Virgin, and Christ; innocent human happiness, human love, and sanctity. None of these seems quite to fit the context, but perhaps mine doesn't either.

sion. It contains these, but they fall within the framework of another theme, for the poem as a whole is a history and in the end a meticulously honest examination of one man's inner change and a weighing of that change to know how great it is, how genuine, how small.

But there is a Lady in *Ash Wednesday*, and she is not quite as negligible as my neglect of her hitherto will have suggested. Like the "kingdoms" in *The Hollow Men*, she, or they, have been variously counted as well as variously identified and explained; but though I remain puzzled on certain points, two considerations frame and probably limit the difficulties. One is the fact that, as was natural following upon his conversion, Eliot had turned to a renewed and intensified study of Dante, with whom he was now deliberately striving to identify himself, learning from him as from a pattern both poetical and spiritual. The other consideration springs from Eliot's personal circumstances, in particular his marriage, for by this time his wife's mental condition, one gathers, had deteriorated beyond hope and in ways most difficult to cope with. The first edition of *Ash Wednesday* bore the dedication "To My Wife," and perhaps from this circumstance a number of readers have been led to identify her in some detail with the Lady, or one of the Ladies. Eliot can easily be imagined wishing, out of kindness, to encourage in his wife herself such a belief if she could bring herself to so construe the situation and the poem. The poem might have been that of a mediaeval penitent sacrificing an earthly love for a spiritual devotion, and there may be a gesture toward this in the line near the beginning, "I renounce the blessed face" (though a different reading of the line is equally possible); or the poem might have been that of the equally traditional lover turning to religion because his Lady has withdrawn herself from him, and there may be a gesture toward this too when the Lady of the leopards "is withdrawn . . . to contemplation."

But *Ash Wednesday* is not really either of these poems, nor is the "Lady" of *Ash Wednesday* either of these women, still less the poet's real wife. *Within the poem* she is a Dantean figure, more Matilda than Beatrice—beautiful, ideal, distant, uttely serene. A heavenly kind of Muse transcending his common humanity, she has no other than a symoblic dimension, being as a person far more abstract and generalized than Beatrice or even Matilda, though as a visual figure she is vivid, flat as in a tapestry. This kind of vividness is one of the gifts upon which Eliot dwelt in the long essay he had just written on Dante, the gift that could create the "Divine Pageant"—Dante's "is a *visual* imagination," Eliot emphasized—with its chariot and its griffin, the scene (*Purgatorio* XXIX-XXX) which Eliot said "belongs to the world of what I call the *high dream.*" In his own vision of Lady and leopards and scattered bones, and later in the procession "between the violet and the violet" of Lady and years and hearse and unicorns he is clearly trying what the modern poetical imagination can do in presicely Dante's manner. His essay quotes and translates the lines introducing Matilda: "A lady alone, who went singing and plucking flower after flower, wherewith her path was pied."[5]

I read, then, as one, the Lady of the leopard scene, she who walked between violets, and the veiled sister who is asked, out of her goodness, to pray for him and who even in her silence makes the fountain spring and the bird sing. She is a serene and a wholly poetical creation, within the poem entirely a fiction. For purely functional reasons Eliot needed some human figure to keep the poem partly in the concrete world; he was not writing an abstract philosophical poem, and one cannot imagine his writing and publishing pure raw confession. Dante's visual imagination pointed the way.

In the development of Eliot's poetry and thought, *Ash Wednesday* is new in more ways than one. The poem is

not a sequel to *The Waste Land*, not even to the individual,
as separated out from the social, aspect of the earlier theme,
for the whole direction of the will in *Ash Wednesday* is
now different, and DA—"give, sympathize, control"—has
very little to do with it. These are not now, in the human
terms in which they were set forth earlier by the thunder,
the means to salvation or even the way to set one's lands
in order preparatory to salvation. The way he has chosen
is subjection of the will to belief and impersonal devotion;
his goal is thus removed not only from humanism but from
human relationships; emphasis has shifted toward the need
for belief, toward ritual and dogma, thus toward the
institutional; this is the kind of change that is examined
in the poem. It is a solitary direction to have taken, and
one not inconceivable for Prufrock.

The Ariel Poems
and *Coriolan*

> This is the time of tension between dying and birth.
>
> *Ash Wednesday* VI

The connection between Prospero's Ariel and the series of Christmas poems by various authors published at a shilling apiece may be explained in some dusty file at Faber and Faber or may not. Eliot, at any rate, wrote an "Ariel" poem each year during the years when *Ash Wednesday* was in progress. Of them all, only the third bears the mark of the occasional poem: *Animula* is competent and dutiful. Dante's discourse on the freedom of the will was at hand, already quoted or about to be quoted in the essay on Dante, which reached the public a fortnight earlier than the poem:

> Issues from the hand of him who fondly loves her ere she is in being, after the fashion of a little child that sports, now weeping, now laughing, the simple, tender soul, who knoweth naught save that, sprung from a joyous maker, willingly she turneth to that which delights her. First she

tastes the savour of a trifling good; there she is beguiled
and runneth after it, if guide or curb turn not her love aside.
Wherefore 'twas needful to put law as a curb, needful to
have a ruler who might discern at least the tower of the
true city.[1]

Eliot filled in this outline with remembered and observed
objects of a child's early life, blending the legs of tables
and chairs and "the fragrant brilliance of the Christmas
tree," with Shakespeare's seven ages of man and Wordsworth's child who recollects his immortality while playing
at being grown up; but Eliot's child, grown up, at death
leaves only "disordered papers in a dusty room," like
Virginia Woolf's Jacob. In following the thought of Dante's
subsequent lines, *Animula* departs from the usual pattern
of Eliot's thought and approaches the Rousseauist doctrine
of natural innocence corrupted by a corrupt society. It
makes little difference that here it is "time" rather than
society that corrupts, as "Issues from the hand of God,
the simple soul" turns into "Issues from the hand of time
the simple soul/ Irresolute and selfish, misshapen, lame,/
Unable to fare forward or retreat." The conclusion however,
somewhat forcibly, carries the theme safely back into the
poet's more usual line of thought. The main attraction
of the poem lies simply in the pleasant, half-affectionate
details of its picture of childhood. The charm was revived
a quarter of a century later when Eliot wrote a still slighter
poem, *The Cultivation of Christmas Trees*, for a new "Ariel"
series, in which the charm is that of fanciful reminiscence,
again an unusual mood for Eliot.

A Song for Simeon, another of Eliot's very few simple
and direct poems, is more substantial and has certain
implications beyond the range of its ostensible persona.
The Simeon of St. Luke's narrative (2: 25-35) and of the
Nunc Dimittis, a "just and devout" man, was promised
by the Holy Ghost that he "should not see death, before
he had seen the Lord's Christ"; and it was granted him

to see the infant Jesus in the Temple. He is then ready
to die in peace, though he knows that many will be in
conflict and that Mary's soul will be pierced by a sword,
for the sake of man's future. As far as he is characterized
in the gospel, he is serene. In language that suggests the
poetical books of the Old Testament rather than the new,
Eliot makes Simeon's virtue specific: "I have ... kept faith
and fast. ... There went never any rejected from my door."
But the poet changes and makes explicit Simeon's vision
of the wider future:

> Who shall remember my house, where shall live my children's
>   children
> When the time of sorrow is come?
> They will take to the goat's path, and the fox's home,
> Fleeing from the foreign faces and the foreign swords.
>
> Before the time of cords and scourges and lamentation
> Grant us thy peace.

This is Israel in the time of Christ, but it is also Europe
in the twentieth century, whether the "foreign swords"
be those from the east of Russia, as *The Waste Land* hinted
or, by now, a renewed Germany or, more generally, the
decay of Europe itself. The spirit of desolation belongs to
Eliot's poem, not to Luke's narrative—a sad spirit for a
public Christmas poem.

Ash Wednesday was a history of spiritual change. *Animula* and, more peripherally, *A Song for Simeon* were
concerned with the theme too. But in the sources of
Journey of the Magi and *Marina*, the two best of the Ariel
poems—inspired, the one by the traditional story of the
Magi, the other by the play of *Pericles*—Eliot found symbols and dramatic personae through which to embody more
particular things he had to say about inner change. They
are more limited in scope than *Ash Wednesday*; at the
same time they are in certain respects even more precise
in embodying their central concern. The truths they illu-

mine are commonplace, amounting to no more than this, that change may be difficult, even severely painful, that one may be reluctant to accept even a desired change. Yet when Eliot has finished with them they have become new truth, with a reality unfelt before.

THE JOURNEY

The suggestion for the first came from a Nativity sermon of Lancelot Andrewes; and what Eliot had said in his essay on Andrewes in introducing a quotation that subsequently became, almost unaltered, the opening lines of the poem, shows that Andrewes's method as well as his theme and language had been useful. "Before extracting all the spiritual meaning of a text," Eliot wrote, "Andrewes forces a concrete presence upon us"; and he quoted Andrewes's passage beginning, "It was no summer progress. A cold coming they had of it," and the rest of what appears, word for word but slightly abridged, as the opening lines of the *Journey.*[2] Accordingly, in the poem Eliot forces upon us a concrete presence and a concrete situation. The whole original conception was Andrewes's, for it was he who had set himself to imagine afresh what the Magi's journey would really have been like, and the folk tradition of easy joy and hope was no part of it, not even so cheerful a spirit as that of the carol "We three kings of Orient are,/ Bearing gifts we come from afar." On the contrary, the journey was hard, "in the dead of winter"; and the sequel was no easier, though this neither Andrewes nor tradition tells us; it is Eliot's own theme.

The journey, presented in concrete, realistic and at the same time partly symbolic detail foreshadowing the Crucifixion—three trees outlined against the sky, hands dicing for silver—is nevertheless also any journey, in any time, today's, almost in today's colloquial prose:

> Then the camel men cursing and grumbling
> And running away, and wanting their liquor and women,
> . . . .
> And the villages dirty and charging high prices.

The journey is marked, though, too, by re-creation of one of those moments when something seen imprints itself upon the memory with a significance that no memory can account for—moments whose inexplicable importance a poet or painter occasionally conveys by no devices that we can explain:

> a water-mill beating the darkness
> . . . .
> a tavern with vine-leaves over the lintel,
> Six hands at an open door dicing for pieces of silver,
> And feet kicking the empty wine-skins.

Eliot spoke of these images in his Conclusion to *The Use of Poetry*. A poet's imagery, he had been saying, "comes from the whole of his sensitive life since early childhood." And he continued:

> Why, for all of us, out of all that we have heard, seen, felt, in a lifetime, do certain images recur, charged with emotion, rather than others? The song of one bird . . . an old woman on a German mountain path, six ruffians seen through an open window playing cards at night at a small French railway junction where there was a water-mill: such memories may have symbolic value, but of what we cannot tell, for they come to represent the depths of feeling into which we cannot peer.[3]

In the poem, these concrete presences that have been so vividly forced upon us end abruptly when the destination is reached. The moment of recognition at the end of the journey is almost omitted, as if it were too sacred for speech: "it was (you may say) satisfactory," Eliot's equivalent for "the rest is silence" though not so grand. There are no gifts and no greetings. The colorless understatement, grossly inadequate on superficial view, serves as a formal sign that the indescribable recognition has occurred. The words have been criticized as a failure on Eliot's part to rise to the occasion, but this is a mistake; it is not an occasion to rise to in language. An attempt to be expressive must have fallen short or rung a false note, and the flat verbal equivalent for a typographical row of periods to signal omission of what is unsayable is in the end more expressive than a futile effort to match speech with the event.

Nothing in Andrewes's sermon or in tradition suggests what follows in the poem as Eliot proceeds to extract what is clearly of primary significance, the sequel that the story omits: for one who has seen the Truth, to live afterwards as a changed man, solitary among familiar but now alien people, is harder than to die.

> There was a Birth, certainly,
> We had evidence and no doubt. I had seen birth and death,
> But had thought they were different; this Birth was
> Hard and bitter agony for us, like Death, our death.
> We returned to our places, these Kingdoms,
> But no longer at ease here, in the old dispensation,
> With an alien people clutching their gods.
> I should be glad of another death.

From the beginning, Eliot had thought of desired change in terms of birth (or life) and death, an obviously natural, universal association representing change in its extreme and inevitable forms. Hence, of course, the constant symbolic use of the paradox in Christian, and not only Christian, thought: *The Golden Bough* and *From Ritual to Romance* are steeped in it. "Death is life and life is death," as Sweeney said. But with Eliot there is in addition always present what does not commonly appear in other handling of the symbols, the consciousness of the pain and difficulty that may be a condition of the change not only when its direction is toward death, but equally when it is toward life, birth, or rebirth: "April is the cruellest month," we remember, and "to say: 'I am Lazarus, come from the dead.'" [a] In the *Journey of the Magi*, the pain of this change is shown, with paradoxical but deadly serious wordplay upon Christ's birth and death and the Magi's own birth to a new life so bitter that "we should be glad of another death." The vividness of the preceding narrative should not obscure this central theme of the poem, the continuing agony of spiritual change.

MARINA

Marina, the fourth of the Ariel poems, bears some relation to the *Journey* in theme, though its poetic method is very different. Like the *Song for Simeon*, the *Journey* is a simply, rather conventionally constructed dramatic monologue in which one of the Magi tells his story pretty much as he really might, in his own voice, aloud; even what Eliot added to the original story for his own purposes reflects a likely outcome of conversion, in the beginning as now. *Marina*, however, is an *interior* monologue heightened into incantatory poetry. None of it would conceivably ever have been said. It is the distillation of moments of a dawning recognition so crucial as to fill a remaining lifetime; it is the anatomy of the moment of change, a moment of oscillation, of alternating retreat and advance toward irrevocable choice between present death and longed-for yet half-dreaded life.

Eliot has been quoted as saying in an unpublished address on Shakespeare that he considered "the finest of all the 'recognition scenes' " in the plays to be that of

[a] There is no indication that in his repeated engagement with this theme Eliot was influenced by psychoanalytic theories of the trauma of birth or the death wish. He must certainly have been aware of the theories but his own formulations of thought bear no resemblance to psychoanalytic formulations.

Act V, scene 1 of "that very great play *Pericles.*"[4] It is difficult not to agree with his judgment of the recognition scene if not of the whole play. The actual story of the partly Shakespearean *Pericles* is a farrago, conspicuous even among Elizabethan plots, of fairly nonsensical improbabilities. Pericles of Tyre, having left his kingdom, sails the seas in desolate mourning for his beloved wife whom he had long before buried at sea, and for his infant daughter Marina, born at sea and now believed dead. In a distant port an unknown girl—Marina, now grown up and escaped from murderer, pirates, and brothel (where she has been bad for the business of the house because no man can bear to harm her, she so purifies the spirits of all who come)—is brought to the ship in one last hope that her beauty and goodness and her lovely singing voice may rouse Pericles from his despair. Unreal in terms of actual characterization, Marina has nevertheless by Shakespearean magic strayed through the play like a wandering ray of light or a transparent angel. Brought before Pericles, she sings, and then speaks of her past. It is, as Eliot said, an unforgettable scene.

In his rendering, the emphasis is changed slightly, in a direction again characteristic of the Eliot of 1930; but the hint is in Shakespeare, where incredulity in Pericles alternates with dawning recognition as Marina tells her story. At one moment he seems half unwilling as well as unable to believe that she is really his living daughter. In Eliot's poem this alternation between willingness and unwillingness to advance becomes the substance of the key lines, the imagery of which—and the oscillation of feeling is presented entirely through images and never otherwise stated—derives from the scene of the play. In the poem, recognition is attended too by a paradoxical but profoundly real mingling of strangeness and familiarity:

What is this face, . . .
The pulse in the arm . . .

> Given or lent? more distant than stars and nearer than the
> eye

As when the subsequent image is echoed in *Murder in the Cathedral* (Part I)—"Voices under sleep, waking a dead world"—the first stirring of recognition comes like voices in a dream, where all "waters meet." Sentence by sentence (Eliot's punctuation is always significant), advance and retreat alternate between the old dead self with frozen soul—the ship, "bowsprit cracked with ice"—and the new soul, "my daughter":

> Bowsprit cracked with ice and paint cracked with heat.
> I made this, I have forgotten
> And remember.
> The rigging weak and the canvas rotten
> Between one June and another September.
> Made this unknowing, half conscious, unknown, my own.
> The garboard strake leaks, the seams need caulking.

Though several of Eliot's eminent critics (Leavis, Helen Gardner, and George Williamson among others) refer "I made this" to the ship, supposing Pericles to say he has built his old ship, such a reading seems to me both improbable and undramatic. "This" is surely his daughter. For one thing, anaphora is continued with unmistakable reference, immediately following the lines I have quoted: "This form, this face." And the alternation, if one follows the periods, is exact: one sentence for the ship (bowsprit cracked . . .), one for the daughter (I made this . . .); again one for the ship (the rigging rotten . . .), and one for the daughter (made this unknowing . . .); the ship (the garboard strake leaks . . .) and finally daughter:

> This form, this face, this life
> Living to live in a world of time beyond me; let me
> Resign my life for this life, my speech for that unspoken,
> The awakened, lips parted, the hope, the new ships.

In these lines recognition is complete and accepted, the

inner change has occurred, the old self with rotten rigging is transformed in "the new ships." There is a clarity in this progression by comparison with which a reading that refers "I made this" to the ship leaves the whole passage shapeless and comparatively meaningless. I emphasize the point because ambivalence in the recognition and rebirth is surely the most distinctive and perceptive feature of the poem's statement. Except for the beautiful incantatory lines at the beginning and end, it is what makes the poem. (The "I made this" formula may owe something to lines in Shakespeare's scene, though the resemblance is not close. Pericles addresses Marina: "O, come hither,/ Thou that beget'st him that did thee beget," followed shortly afterwards by "Rise; thou art my child./ Give me fresh garments"—"the new ships").

Through the epigraph from Seneca's *Hercules Furens*, Eliot introduces another dramatic recognition antithetical to that of *Pericles*. It is the scene in which Hercules recovers from madness inflicted by Hera, during which he has killed his wife and children. He awakens, at first not knowing where he is (*"Quis hic locus . . ."*), to recognition of the horror he has committed. Eliot explained that he used the two recognition scenes in order to form a "crisscross" between Pericles, who finds the living, and Hercules, who finds the dead.[5] One can speculate upon further meanings possibly conferred upon the poem by the *Hercules*—a reminder, perhaps, that one may awaken to Hell as well as to Heaven, or a reminder, not explicitly pointed out by the Pericles story, that the old self has been a sinful self—but the allusion to the *Hercules* does not get caught up into the poem. Even the opening line, which partly echoes the Senecan line, is translated from the terrestrial scene of Hercules' awakening to the marine of Pericles (and of Massachusetts), seas, shores, rocks, islands, fog. Once one knows the context of the epigraph, the allusion injects a little grit into what might be conceived as a too smoothly happy conclusion; in life one does have to live with the consequences of one's past, which the Pericles of the play in the end does not. In this way, peripheral though it is, the allusion perhaps has the value of casting a vague sort of shadow over the whole.

The poem contains one passage, however, that no amount of effort on my part enables me to feel as anything but an intrusion. The beautiful lyric opening is followed by eight stiffly formal, oracular lines in a different, often huddled rhythm (huddled as in a chant when the congregation sings many words to one note) and spoken in a voice which is not the sublimated inner voice of Pericles that speaks the rest of the poem; nor is it in any other pertinent voice that Eliot marshals some four of the seven deadly sins, all "meaning Death." Inescapably, this is the voice of the Preacher intruding. The passage must, I suppose, be meant to register unequivocally, in case it should be mistaken, the fact that the recognition and turning toward life that follow are to be understood in a specifically Christian sense. Both the imagery and the statements, however, as well as the style of the passage, force upon us something that does not grow naturally out of the rest of the poem. Eliot may have hoped that through his old cinematic technique of abrupt juxtapositions a link not explicit would be felt and an effect created something like that of the Thunder's voice speaking DA in *The Waste Land*. But it is not like that, because the poet's own imagination is felt to be absorbed, as the reader's is, for the duration of the poem in the pure process of recognition and change as distilled out of the moments in the play. The scene does not read like allegory but like broader symbolism: there has been no abstraction and no doctrine walking naked looking to Shakespeare's play for clothes. The scene itself is at the center, and only through the depth of its own realization does it become the type of all recognition involving change. The poem thus unites

something narrower than the Christian church, the drama
of a personal recognition, and something more universal—
the experience of subjective change itself—leaving the
oracular voice of the preacher with its list of arbitrarily
selected sins a false note, a perfunctory insertion:

> Those who sit in the sty of contentment, meaning
> Death
> Those who suffer the ecstasy of the animals, meaning
> Death

—and so on. Even so, even, that is, granting so serious
a flaw as this appears to me, *Marina* stands among Eliot's
memorable achievements.

CORIOLAN

At the end of 1930 Eliot told G. Wilson Knight that
he was writing "a poem inspired by Beethoven's *Coriolan*"
(Knight's words). Behind the music was the play, and he
asked to see Knight's newly finished essay on Shakespeare's
Coriolanus.[6] The appearance of Eliot's "Triumphal
March," not very suitably, as a fifth Ariel poem in 1931
must then have been a matter simply of convenience, for
in that poem Eliot was already on his way to something
different and larger. After *Ash Wednesday* and the other
highly subjective Ariel poems, he now returned to the
external world in this first of the two parts of *Coriolan*;
and the subject returned him also to a rhythm of drumbeats, which reappear, but with the kinaesthetic music-hall
rhythms of *Sweeney Agonistes* now transformed into a
heavier military march. The use of a similar beat in the
frame of *The Hollow Men* with its otherwise weak music
of *fin de siècle* dejection, had made the rhythm there seem
the deliberate imposition of a forcible cure for tired verse.
Now, in the recent poems following his conversion, there
had been no such weakness. They are highly introspective,

however, and for the most part loftily poetical in style; and *Coriolan* represents a reaction toward the external world, toward the concerns that had been occupying Eliot's prose, and toward a flat prosaic manner suggesting *Sweeney* again but less stylized, less brittle.

Technically, in *Coriolan* the drumbeat, now sparingly used, alternates with a blank verse more energetic and much freer than before, but at times it drops into pure prose that maintains only the line divisions of verse. The whole of *Coriolan*, however, as far as it was written, represents for Eliot a new departure to which its metrical structure makes only a minor contribution, for the poem is dominated by its theme and by the exceptional range of tones or voices brought to bear, within so short a space, upon the theme. Though not literally in dramatic form like *Sweeney Agonistes*, *Coriolan* is the work of a poet moving toward playwriting.

There had been range enough of voices in *The Waste Land*, where they occurred mainly in discrete blocks. In *Coriolan*, one voice leads into another through stretches of perfectly flat, characterless language, unlike the stylized flat speech in *Sweeney Agonistes*. These passages have no style at all except for one parenthesis spoken by "Cyril's" mother, who may as well be Lil's friend revived for the occasion, "Don't throw away that sausage,/ It'll come in handy. He's artful."

> Stone, bronze, stone, steel, stone, oakleaves, horses' heels
> Over the paving.
> And the flags. And the trumpets. And so many eagles.
> How many? Count them. And such a press of people.

The characterless flatnes in lines like the last, representing the gaping spectators' composite meaningless perceptions, alternates with lines of Christian symbolism in heightened verse: "Under the palmtree ... / At the still point of the turning world." The essential dialogue—to stretch a point in calling it that—in "Triumphal March" is between poet and spectators; in the second part of *Coriolan*, "Difficulties of a Statesman," it takes place between the tormented self of Coriolanus—his sense of the external pressures upon him heard as voices ringing in his mind—and again the poet.

Two figures, one of them his own creation, fascinated Eliot over a period of years. Whether it is Sweeney or Coriolanus that represents his Yeatsian anti-self or its psychoanalytical equivalent I leave to those more closely in touch with Eliot's unconscious or with psychoanalytical theory to say. Certainly, Sweeney represents all that the known Eliot was not, and something he might at times have half wished to be; we do not forget the boxing lessons. And it can be argued that the object of a strong wish, and not the wish only, is part of the self. Yet, however we place Sweeney, it is at all events certain that the figure of Coriolanus symbolizes in a very different way something that *was* a functional part of the known Eliot even though it is not—or not now—possible to know precisely all that the actual play of Shakespeare or its protagonist represented for him. When writing in 1919 of "Hamlet and His Problems" and finding that play unsatisfactory, he had named *Coriolanus*, in an equally idiosyncratic judgment, as, "with *Antony and Cleopatra*, Shakespeare's most assured artistic success" and had even maintained that the series of "tragic successes" following *Hamlet* "culminate in *Coriolanus*."[7]

> I shall not want Honour in Heaven
>> For I shall meet Sir Philip Sidney
> And have talk with Coriolanus
>> And other heroes of that kidney.

These jaunty lines from *A Cooking Egg*, also written in 1919, are answered in that earlier poem by a cry of

disillusion, "Where are the eagles and the trumpets?" and
the high symbols of triumph are brought to earth with
a mixture of the sad and the flip:

> Buried beneath some snow-deep Alps.
> Over buttered scones and crumpets
> Weeping, weeping multitudes
> Droop in a hundred A. B. C.'s.

Now in the *Coriolan* of 1931 more than a decade later,
Eliot chose to repeat his impudent rhyme of *trumpets* and
crumpets, but the ironic tone has deepened in the interval.
Again, in 1919 it had been Coriolanus who uttered the
malediction introducing the *Ode* of *Ara Vos Prec*. And
in the climactic division of *The Waste Land*, Coriolanus
is "broken" in the prison of the self. The figure is pivotal
there. "Each in his prison/ Thinking of the key, each
confirms a prison"; yet under the command of the Thunder,
"Dayadhvam"—"sympathize" (an inadequate translation;
something larger is meant)—"at nightfall, aethereal ru-
mours/ Revive for a moment a broken Coriolanus."

Eliot's own arrogance was real, not mere defensive
bluster, and its influence on his creative work was by no
means all negative. Partly to it we owe the daring original-
ity of the poems beginning, paradoxically, with his portrait
of the timid self of Coriolanus's antithesis Prufrock ("I
am not [even] Prince Hamlet"). But the arrogance speaks
out most clearly in the tone of much of Eliot's prose,
increasingly so through the first years of his religious
conversion, and is neither modified nor disguised by the
occasional cursory expressions of modesty. These were the
years, again paradoxically, when *Ash Wednesday* reveals
a struggle for Christian humility only less urgent than
the struggle for belief. Afterwards, in passage after passage,
Murder in the Cathedral reflects with sympathy and
without implied criticism the protagonist's arrogant pride
of power both worldly and spiritual. In the Coriolanus of

Shakespeare pride was broken through the hero's attachment to his strong-willed mother. In Eliot, who, perhaps
incidentally and perhaps not, is also understood to have
been deeply attached to his strong-willed mother (she had
died in 1929, the year before *Coriolan* was begun), the
arrogance seems ultimately not to have been subdued
either by love or by the Christian ideal but to have half
transformed itself through identification with the impersonal authoritarianism of his politics and religion. This
is where the poem *Coriolan* enters.

Too little of it was written to enable us to guess what
the final work might have become. Eliot is quoted as having
said in 1950 that it was to have shown "a sequence in
the life of the character who appears in this first part as
"Young Cyril";[8] but this does not take us very far with
the Coriolanus theme itself, which dominates the existing
"Triumphal March" and "Difficulties of a Statesman."
Imagery from Shakespeare's play, its express contempt for
the populace and magnification of the heroic leader, Coriolanus's own arrogance, and perhaps much, perhaps little,
of the more individual elements of his tragedy, are all
marshalled in Eliot's fragments, but they are marshalled
in the service of a theme rather different, that of the state
of England and Europe in 1930 and 1931.

In an article of December 1928 in *Criterion*, "The Literature of Fascism," an article not defending Fascism but also
not treating it with noticeable severity, Eliot had written,
"Possibly also, hidden in many breasts ['O hidden under
the dove's wing, hidden in the turtle's breast,' as we read
in *Coriolan*] is a craving for a regime which will relieve
us of thought and at the same time give us excitement
and military salutes."[9] This might have been but is not
quite the motto for the "Triumphal March," for in the
poem Eliot says, quoting Edmund Husserl, "The natural
wakeful life of our Ego is a perceiving," and the crowd
watching the procession are not so much cheering or

rejoicing (one is not conscious of a "craving" being satisfied) as they are simply looking on—naming and counting—as the spoils of war wheel by, spoils which in literal fact are made up from a list of matériel surrendered by the Germans after Versailles, gained at the cost of a generation of young Englishmen. The hero at their head, too, in the poem is "perceiving"; he is not triumphant:

> There is no interrogation in his eyes
> Or in the hands, quiet over the horse's neck,
> And the eyes watchful, waiting, perceiving, indifferent.

Not, on the whole, a pleasant series of adjectives; and the drift of the passage is to me uncertain. It is followed immediately by the lines of clear Christian reference which conclude:

> O hidden under the dove's wing, hidden in the turtle's breast,
> Under the palmtree at noon, under the running water
> At the still point of the turning world. O hidden

—a passage serving as a reminder of that other procession, Christ's entry into Jerusalem. Probably it is right to suppose we are being told that this Coriolan figure is not the saviour needed but the pseudo-saviour deserved; that though still, he is not the still point of the turning world. But the figure and the epithets describing him are equivocal, and the meaning may, instead, be a question: Is this abstracted, impenetrable figure of the leader, not Christ, of course, but what the present politico-historical world needs and never understands? [b] Even the symbolic eagle and dove, however, are equivocal; the most familiar lines

[b] As in the *Gerontion* volume and *The Waste Land*, allusive imagery from the past is drawn from various sources, the most significant being the probable reference to the entry into Jerusalem. Discussions in Smith, *Eliot's Poetry*, pp. 159-167, and Kenner, *Invisible Poet*, pp. 158-160 present most of the sources. Their discussions, however, perhaps merely because they assume that the reader will take it for granted, tend to ignore what is implied in the figure of Coriolanus himself.

in Shakespeare's play are those of Coriolanus's last desperate boast before he is killed, "Like an eagle in a dove-cote,
I/ Flutter'd your Volscians in Corioli;/ Alone I did it,"
lines which Eliot later borrowed for Becket's boast (in
Murder in the Cathedral Part I), "I who ruled like an
eagle over doves."

Eliot's Coriolan is above all solitary; but his crowd, too,
in a curious way is solitary. And, in other terms, the
populace is so far from the still point, "young Cyril" so
ignorant of its meaning that, taken to church on Easter
Sunday for no better reason than that "we didn't get to
the country" that day, he mistakes the bell rung at the
elevation of the Host for that of the muffin-and-crumpets
vendor, and so Eliot gets his rhyme again, *trumpets* and
crumpets. At the end, as any man in the crowd may ask
another:

> Please will you
> Give us a light?

we hear the meaning of the pun without altogether com-
prehending its implications:

> Light
> Light
> *Et les soldats faisaient la haie? ILS LA FAISAIENT.* [c]

In the ethical implications of its conclusion, Shakespeare's
own *Coriolanus* is more complex and indeterminate than
most of the tragedies. In most there is an Aristotelian
catharsis, some recognition of values, a voice of understanding somewhere to be heard. In *Coriolanus*, at least
as today we ordinarily read the play, the values remain
confused; and in this very confusion lies the essence of
its tragedy—or of its failure as a tragedy, in the view of

---

[c] The line is from Maurras's *L'Avenir de l'intelligence*. Matthiessen,
pp. 82-83, has a particularly good discussion of the influence of this book,
even stylistically, on *Coriolan*.

many readers. Eliot never referred to this central aspect
of the play.

Nineteen-thirty was the year of economic crisis in the
Western world, touched off by the financial panic of 1929
in the United States. In the German elections of 1930,
the Nazi party first became a major force, increasing its
representation in the Reichstag from 12 to 104. Rosenberg's
The Myth of the Twentieth Century appeared in 1930 with
its attacks upon Christianity, Western civilization, and
European tradition. All over England, the dearth of competent leadership was being laid to the death in 1914-1918
of those who should have been its future leaders. After
the general election of 1929, with Ramsay McDonald again
Prime Minister, diplomatic relations with Russia were
resumed; in 1931 the Bank of England and the pound
reached a crisis . . . *a coalition government was formed.*
. . . "Difficulties of a Statesman":

> The Order of the Black Eagle (1st and 2nd class),
> And the Order of the Rising Sun.
> Cry cry what shall I cry?
> *The first thing to do is to form the committees* [my italics]:
> . . . .
> A commission is appointed
> To confer with a Volscian commission
> About perpetual peace: . . .
> Meanwhile the guards shake dice on the marches
> . . . .
> Mother mother
> . . . .
> O mother
> What shall I cry?
> We demand a committee, . . .
> RESIGN   RESIGN   RESIGN

These are the outer dimensions of the second part of
Coriolan. Within and between its parts are introduced
contrasting hints of spiritual peace, beneath the breast of

the dove, the still moment with no eagles or trumpets.

Underlying the whole of *Coriolan*, then, as far as it goes, is this complex of public disintegration, degradation of the populace, the need of a leader, the need of religion public and private—all interwoven with allusion to the Shakespearean epitome of arrogance, the general with broken will subject to his mother. And through the tone of the whole runs a subjective sense of identification with this leader. Eliot's fragment never got to the end of Shakespeare's play, where Aufidius says, "Beat the drum, that it speak mournfully," the stage direction concluding with the words "A dead march sounded." Which is where Beethoven enters.

It is curious that the figures of Sweeney and Coriolanus, whatever each meant to Eliot, are the two that were never carried through into the completed works which Eliot projected for them. From the standpoint of his development as a poet, both proved dead ends, his only published fragments. The plan to create out of Sweeney a subtle double-speaker of significant truths presented possibly insurmountable obstacles. *Coriolan*, however, hasn't the same appearance of a self-terminating project; in it, as far as the reader can see, Eliot had not, or not yet, boxed himself in, though its direction remains obscure. Thereafter Eliot's poetical dealings with men and women in the external world were to be carried on through the series of plays; the poems would return to their more subjective element. We hear no more of Coriolanus; he is replaced in drama by the martyr Becket, who utters many lines that might have been his.

9

The Pattern Is Ironed into the Carpet

You say I am repeating
Something I have said before. I shall say it again.
East Coker III

The order, the form, the texture of my books will perhaps some day constitute for the initiated a complete representation. . . ."the string the pearls were strung on, the buried treasure, the figure in the carpet.
(Hugh Vereker in James's ironical story
"The Figure in the Carpet")

One day a descendant of Caroline Spurgeon will approach Eliot's poems with a computer in hand; and Lazarus will then return from the dead to tell us All. In the meantime.—

Though Eliot obviously had the natural poet's gift for language, his was not one of the superlative verbal imaginations in English poetry. His does not compare with the imaginative power of Yeats for the daring and resonant word or line, or for the dramatic ordering of syntax. The scarcely explicable magnificence of "that dolphin-torn, that gong-tormented sea" was beyond Eliot; so, even, was the line closing Yeats's early *Cuchulain's Fight with the Sea* (in its revised version), where the effect is centered in the strung-out length, as well as the resonance, of one word, "And fought with the invulnerable tide," through which memory of the literal sense of "invulnerable" floods the line with the irony of all that has gone before in the poem. These are but two of countless instances. In this particular kind of genius Yeats was perhaps inferior only to Shakespeare, who achieved similar effects often with less spectacular material—Cleopatra's "there is nothing left remarkable/ Beneath the visiting moon," for example, with the restrained, as it was then, understatement of "remarkable" and all the impermanence of life and value concentrated in the simple, startling epithet "visiting." Or the line, made up of even more ordinary units taken separately, which Eliot (misquoting) cited as so highly poetical, "Put up your bright swords or the dew will rust them." [a] The comparison is unfair to Eliot, but smaller poets have had the gift too in their degree, de la Mare, for example. Eliot's language has not the utter verbal felicity of a breath-taking flight that still lands so exactly on its feet; his language gains its resonance, instead, through its tones and firm texture, its imagery and traditional allusiveness, through the poet's fine ear for cadence and timing, and finally, through the patterns of recurrence in which an image becomes enriched by its past and future contexts.

RECURRENT IMAGES

During the years between about 1928 and 1930—whether by chance or not, the years immediately following his

---

[a] "Keep up your bright swords, for the dew will rust them" (*Othello* I.2.59). Eliot's misquotation (in the essay of 1929 on Dante) was pointed out to me by Professor Irwin Griggs.

religious conversion—several influences came together to crystallize certain things which Eliot as poet and critic had already been half aware of and half practicing. The "Impersonal theory of poetry," which he had proclaimed in 1919, had never been tenable in all its purity, and, as we know, Eliot's views on the subject changed over the years. As late as 1927, however, in his address before the Shakespeare Association on "Shakespeare and the Stoicism of Seneca," though he now said unequivocally that "what every poet starts from is his own emotions," he was still wary of what is not quite the same thing as emotion, "personality." Through most of that essay he is engaged in setting up Seneca as an antidote for the purpose of destroying the various "personalities" of Shakespeare created by Lytton Strachey, Middleton Murry, Wyndham Lewis, and earlier by Coleridge and Swinburne—a Shakespeare, he observed, created by each writer in his own image. And Eliot in 1927 is still not interested in finding the "real" personality of Shakespeare, "if there is one," he says.[1]

His renewed study of Dante, however (who had transformed a chaotic life into a pattern), resulted in the long essay of 1929 which compared the two great poets and advocated a study of Shakespeare's plays, "taken in order," in the hope of interpreting "the pattern in Shakespeare's carpet"; and in the next year, again with reference to Shakespeare, he remarked that "by 'work of art' I mean here rather the work of one artist as a whole."[2] Finally, in 1932, in the passage quoted at the beginning of this study, Eliot asserted the belief that what "matters most" in weighing the greatness of a poet is "this unity in a lifetime's work," that the whole of Shakespeare's work "is *one* poem ... united by one significant, consistent, and developing personality"; this, he added, "is one of the measures of major poetry and drama." By this time such unity had clearly become his own conscious goal as a poet (perhaps he was now thinking "major" poet), and "person-ality" had become a key element in the "pattern." In the same essay he refers to the work of Wilson Knight.

For many years Eliot had been in touch with contem-porary studies of Shakespeare and other Elizabethans, not only with purely literary studies outside the universities such as those of Murry and Wyndham Lewis, but with academic studies also. He had addressed the Shakespeare Association in 1927, as Caroline Spurgeon did in 1930. Her massive study of Shakespeare's imagery did not appear till 1935, but it had been in progress for some years, was based on work made public much earlier, and was well known before the completed work appeared. Meanwhile, part of Wilson Knight's work was taking the same direction. In 1928 or early 1929, Eliot made the acquaintance of both the writing and person of Knight; he knew Knight's *Myth and Miracle* (1929) [b] and took sufficient interest in his line of thought to arrange for publication by Oxford of *The Wheel of Fire* in 1930 and to write an introduction for it. In that year also, reading in manuscript (at his own request) Knight's then unpublished essay on *Coriolanus*, Eliot was most of all impressed, he said, by "the detailed and convincing analysis of the type of imagery." [c] He was attracted, then, to the Shakespearean studies which were turning toward analysis of imagery and "what it tells us"

[b] See Knight's recollections in Tate, pp. 245-261. It may have been this work, later republished as *The Crown of Life*, that drew Eliot's particular attention to the play of *Pericles*, to which Knight gives high praise at the beginning of his book.

[c] *Ibid.*, pp. 247-248, quoting from Eliot's letter. Knight has more to say about imagery here than in much of his other early work. He emphasizes the hard and the metallic imagery in *Coriolanus*—"even fish may have metallic fins," he says, and cites the lead, stone, flint, oak, and so on throughout the play (*The Imperial Theme* [London: Methuen, 1961], p. 155, first published in 1931; cf. Eliot's opening line). Knight's discussion of imagery is always associated with his analysis of the theme and, of course, with "the whole" of Shakespeare. The mystical side of Knight's thought was not at the time so much to Eliot's purpose.

of the poet's themes, attitudes, and personality, when related images recur within a play or a particular period, or throughout the whole of a lifetime's work.

Eliot needed no more than the hint before he should set out systematically to construct for himself a unified and "developing" poetic personality, set out, evidently, to create "*one* poem" out of his whole work; and this new intention perceptibly affects much of the poetry that followed, though it is an intensification of what he was already doing rather than a sharp change of direction: he had not far to go from where he had already been. What he had always had to work with was a limited range of sensibility, limited emotional range, a limited internal storehouse of imagery that had emotional meaning, and an over-riding concern with one theme, the possibility for the self or the world of "breeding lilacs out of the dead land." The other side of the fabric of limitation is unity, and Eliot's temperament had thus already conferred a high degree of unity upon his themes and his imagery.

It is evident that, from 1930 or before, he was directing attention to the deliberate creation of a "whole" pattern of this imagery, taking material from his earlier poems and suitably altering it to reflect the changing or "developing personality" of the present poet as he conceived him to be. The result is sometimes happy, sometimes frigid; but in either case the effect of the deliberateness itself upon the texture of his writing, noticeably different from that of unconscious or half-conscious recurring patterns in the work of most poets, is marked. A skimming view of two or three of the many threads will illustrate the point.

Two particular groups of images have long been recognized as peculiarly Eliot's, those associated with drought and those with eyes: they are the continuing symbolic images in his work which seem most rooted in direct experience and least spun out of literary associations, though both, especially the first, also have a rich history in tradition. Drought had been implicit, not named, in *Prufrock; Gerontion* begins and ends with it—the old man "in a dry month" and the "thoughts of a dry brain in a dry season"; it turns up briefly also in other poems of 1917-1919: even in *Mr. Eliot's Sunday Morning Service* "the wilderness is cracked and browned" though the service presumably takes place at home in England. The expression "dried up" occurs repeatedly in the prose and the speech of Eliot, particularly with reference to himself; but he early knew also a "distinguished aridity" when he saw it. In *The Waste Land*, of course, this image becomes the controlling symbol, and it remains at the center through the straw, the "dried voices," the cactus land of *The Hollow Men* and after, till in *Ash Wednesday*, at the point where the symbol reaches its extreme limit, its nature is transformed and it becomes beneficent. The bones scattered in the desert are now glad: having had to construct something upon which to rejoice, they rejoice; and the desert is ready to give way to the garden, of which a fore-glimpse is given as the bones sing their hymn. It is a neatly rounded history.

Beginning with *Prufrock* and the *Portrait of a Lady*, eyes and passages associated with them, like drought, make their appearance as objective correlatives for significant feeling. The most intense of these, the eyes that "fix" you like an impaled insect, flanked by the twin moments in which you "prepare a face to meet the faces that you meet," only to discover ("turning shall remark/ Suddenly, [your] expression in a glass") that what you have prepared is a strained grimace—this group of images focuses much of whatever feeling there is in the early work. As his mood changed in the volume that followed *Prufrock*, though eyes are not a dominant image, when they do appear they again focus much of the feeling of that time, calling forth Eliot's most grotesque language. They are always others' eyes, and they are all detestable. They stare, and one would

not like to be looked at by them: Bleistein's "lustreless
protrusive eye/ Stares from the protozoic slime," and even
Seraphim *stare* in the poet's Sunday Morning Service. In
Whispers of Immortality, "daffodil bulbs instead of balls/
Stared from the sockets of the eyes"—a grotesque parody
of the rose and ivy that used to spring from lovers' graves
in ballads or of the irreverent but inoffensive slang of
"pushing daisies." The most familiar quoted line in *The
Waste Land* comes from the song in which Shakespeare's
fancy had transmuted death by water into beauty: the
bones are coral, "those are pearls that were his eyes." As
Eliot's poem now stands, the line occurs twice in contexts
that are ambiguous but that at any rate are not gross
distortions. In a "Dirge," however, which appears to have
been one of the poems Pound discouraged Eliot from
inserting in *The Waste Land*, the grotesque is altogether
out of control. There it is Bleistein who lies "full fathom
five," and there are no pearls, only the staring eyes of goiter:
"Graves' Disease in a dead jew's eyes!/ Where the crabs
have eat the lids"[3] (this, with the rest of the "Dirge," may
be the lowest depth to which Eliot's taste sank in those
disturbed years).

   Within the partial opacity of *The Hollow Men* and the
minor "eyes" lyric associated with it, we have glimpses
of eyes that are one's own as well as those of others from
which one shrinks: imaginary eyes that have become
beneficent but only so through a dream of escape; eyes
that might be transformed into the multifoliate rose of
the *Paradiso* but will not be because Paradise does not
exist. The most real in this welter of eyes are those the
hollow man dare not meet in dreams, the accusing self-
projections of a guilt that is now deeper than the self-consciousness which had been the meaning of the eyes Prufrock
feared. The twisting and turning of the image from poem
to poem and within *The Hollow Men* itself is deliberate.
Even this is not quite, however, what Eliot began to do

in another four or five years; and within *The Hollow Men* alone the imagery is handled rather in the manner of the seventeenth-century conceit, suggesting Donne and Herbert and more particularly Lancelot Andrewes with their serious ingenuity of play upon language and imagery.[4]

Till about 1929 or possibly 1930 these patterns and continuities are little more than we should expect from this particular poet with his particular ritualistic and form-loving temperament and limitations: one would guess the patterns, *as* patterns, to be sometimes half-conscious and sometimes thoroughly conscious but in either case a natural way of thinking and imagining, not part of a calculated system directed to a clearly defined end. The change in their character was apparently touched off by the current critical studies to which I have referred, pointing to unity of imagery and symbol in Shakespeare's works and to the light shed by these patterns upon our whole conception of what constitutes the developing "personality" of Shakespeare. The effect begins to show toward the end of *Ash Wednesday*—"The desert in the garden the garden in the desert"—and becomes a marked device in *Coriolan*. After the poetic drought that followed—Eliot wrote virtually nothing but prose between 1931 and late 1933—the device is pervasive. From that time on, out of his own poems and plays he was deliberately creating the "one poem" which should be "the whole of Eliot." In practice, this involved consecutively related themes marking a development and made concrete through repetitive patterns of symbolic imagery—nothing so very unusual except the conscious and systematic pursuit of it and the marks of that thorough-going deliberateness upon the work itself. After *Ash Wednesday*, to take one of the major transformations, the desert vanishes from the poetry except for brief occasions when it enters, usually, as an admonishment to others, not to oneself (as in *The Rock* I). For oneself it is replaced by the rose garden of *Burnt Norton*, which remains the controlling image even through the destruction of war—"Ash on an old man's sleeve/ Is all the ash the burnt roses leave"—for in the end "the fire and the rose are one."

The eyes too have a further history. Those of the Prufrockian self-consciousness are transformed in the same rose garden of *Burnt Norton*, where instead of shrinking before the eyes of the beholder the flower glows with pleasure, "the roses/ Had the look of flowers that are looked at": the image seems deliberately invented for the purpose of exorcising the eyes that had afflicted Prufrock, for it has otherwise no function in the scene. The spiritual history of the others, the accusing eyes fixing guilt, was carried to a separate conclusion: it reached both its climax of horror and its reconciliation in the Eumenides of *The Family Reunion*. "Do you like to be stared at by eyes through a window?" Harry asks. He had known "they" were coming "in the Java Straits, in the Sunda Sea,/ In the sweet sickly tropical night"; in Italy, "from behind the nightingale's thicket,/ The eyes stared at me, and corrupted that song" (Part I, scene 1). Harry has murdered his wife or else fancies he has murdered her; the ambiguity itself is the meaning, for beneath its Aeschylean formulation the theme is original sin and Harry, who is Man, is by definition guilty; he knows that whatever he has or has not done, the pursuing eyes, the Furies are not to be eluded. In the end of this allegory they are exorcised by Harry's ceasing to flee them and turning toward some unnamed ultimate sacrifice. After this, as far as I can remember, symbolic eyes disappear from Eliot's poetry.

Among the more purely traditional, impersonal symbols of which Eliot also makes patterns, that of the ancient protean wheel is ubiquitous. Bussy d'Ambois's axle-tree of heaven shattered to atoms in *Gerontion* sinks to earth as the axle-tree of Mallarmé's mud in *Burnt Norton*; the spiritual still point in the turning world of *Ash Wednesday*

reappears from time to time; the ship's wheel turned by
Phlebas is recollected in *Murder in the Cathedral*; the
spiritual "turning" played upon by Lancelot Andrewes
provides the "turning" frame for *Ash Wednesday*: these
are but the least skimming of Eliot's wheels and their still
points. In *Coriolan* the poet went back to *A Cooking Egg*
for his eagles and trumpets and crumpets, to Burbank and
his Princess for the cry which originally had signaled
the King's guilt in *Hamlet*, the cry for "Light/Light."
In *Coriolan* a request, it is afterwards in *The Rock* (ix)
transformed into a promise of spiritual "Light/Light." And
Coriolan returns to *Ash Wednesday* for the "still point
of the turning world," to *Journey of the Magi* for soldiers
shaking dice while great events pass them by. For the
choruses in *The Rock* Eliot systematically rifled his earlier
work; they are a tissue of calculated echoes joined to a
few anticipations of work to come: from *Coriolan* the
setting up of "commissions" and the "resigning"; from *The
Waste Land*, "Oed' und leer das Meer" translated into
a refrain: "Waste and void. Waste and void. And darkness
on the face of the deep" (vii). And so on.

From that time forward, sometimes natural, sometimes
forced, patterned echoes are a constant feature of Eliot's
work. As in *The Waste Land*, so in *The Family Reunion*,
spring "is the time/ For the ache in the moving root/ The
agony in the dark/ ... / The pain of the breaking bud";
twice in *East Coker* we are reminded of Prufrock's patient
etherized upon a table. A further catalogue is not needed.
Readers thoroughly familiar with the later work will
already have become aware of the echoes that prevail
everywhere; those less familiar with it may play the game
at will. Short of a computer with human sensibilities, they
are close to being countless; and I think in the long run
Eliot rather ran this form of recurrence and continuity
into the ground, though many of the occasional effects
are superb. Patterns once natural have become studied,

and when the poem or passage is otherwise imaginatively impoverished, the calculated echoes ensure its sterility. Whether individually successful or not, the body of imagery as a whole bears weight, however, for in it is concentrated the conscious history of the poet's inner self insofar as he was willing to project it in the poems. What he possibly failed to take into account is an inevitable rigidity in patterns pursued with such systematic determination in the *construction* of a poetic personality. [d]

TWO "LANDSCAPES"

Apart from *The Rock*, which is long but poetically negligible, only two of the five short "Landscape" poems distinguish the four-year interval between "Difficulties of a Statesman" and the composition of *Burnt Norton*, one of them, *New Hampshire*, notable chiefly because it is the focus for Eliot's happiest cluster of images, the other, *Rannoch, by Glencoe*, mainly on its own account as a lyric though it too is interwoven with other poems in the pattern of Eliot's symbolic imagery.

New Hampshire presents the fullest version of a group of images which functions in some respects (but not altogether) like the rose garden, as an antithesis to the waste

[d] Returning to his old imagery, Eliot seems to have undertaken, in passing, to validate retroactively one or two images that he had originally introduced rather irresponsibly, probably "because they sounded well," as he confessed in his lecture on Seneca and Shakespeare: the "shadow of this red rock" in *The Waste Land*, which used to send scholars on vain chases for source or symbol, is given naturalistic meaning retrospectively in the conclusion of *Murder in the Cathedral*, though its origin, we now know, was in an equally naturalistic but different context, describing firelight on the walls of a cave (*WL Facs.*, p. [91]); the "blue vain chases for source or symbol, is given naturalistic meaning retrospectively in the conclusion of *Murder in the Cathedral*, though its origin, is descriptively naturalized in *The Rock* III. For a study of recurrent image and symbol in Eliot's later work, see Louis Martz, "The Wheel and the Point: Aspects of Imagery and Theme in Eliot's Later Poetry," *Sewanee Review*, LV (1947), 126-147.

desert: Children's voices, laughter among leaves, blossoming trees, birds:

> Children's voices in the orchard
> Between the blossom- and the fruit-time:
> Golden head, crimson head,
> Between the green tip and the root.

Perhaps because in the line "Golden head, crimson head" I hear, incorrigibly, only Joyce—"Bronze by gold, Miss Douce's head by Miss Kennedy's head" in the Ormond Bar—I have never thought the poem as fine a lyric as many do. But the images together are not of course Joyce. They appear significantly after Eliot's conversion, first as hints in *Ash Wednesday*, then more fully in *Marina*, "Whispers and small laughter between leaves and hurrying feet." [e] They reappear with the First Tempter in *Murder in the Cathedral* (Part I), "Laughter and apple-blossom floating.... Singing at nightfall, whispering ..." and most vividly in *Burnt Norton*:

> Go, said the bird, for the leaves were full of children,
> Hidden excitedly, containing laughter,

and again at the close, the moment of happiness, "hidden laughter/ Of children in the foliage.... Ridiculous the waste sad time/ Stretching before and after"; and there is one final echo, "children in the apple-tree," at the end of *Little Gidding* and of Eliot's poetry itself.

The images, which are unlike anything else in Eliot, shed their light here and there through the later poems, suggesting, as Dame Helen Gardner says, "an image of human happiness,"[5] and a little more too if their main origin is as I think, the fairy story of Oscar Wilde, "The Selfish

---

[e] Their very first appearance in Eliot's poetry, however, is in the context deriving from Catallus's boys in the *Ode* of *Ara Vos Prec*, a meaning and a context for which I have no explanation, other than perhaps an accident of phrasing.

Giant" (in *The Happy Prince*), a story which most readers of Eliot's age and background would have known and which, once known, is not easily forgotten. Conrad Aiken, in the days of his earlier friendship with Eliot at Harvard and abroad, actually "memorized," he tells us, Wilde's "little fairy stories."[6] In this one, children play in the giant's garden among the birds and flowers and peach trees till the absent Giant comes home and walls them out. No spring comes then in the garden, no song of birds, and the trees remain bare. After barren years have passed, the Giant hears a linnet's song: the children have crept in through a hole in the wall and now each is sitting in the branches of a tree, which have all suddenly broken into bloom, except for one still bare tree with a boy beneath too small to climb. The repentant Giant lifts the child, and his tree too breaks into bloom. This smallest child is never seen again till the Giant is old and dying; then his tree breaks into bloom though the season is midwinter, and the child is there with marks of nails in hands and feet, to lead the Giant to His garden of Paradise. It is a touching fairy story, simply told; and something of its spirit seems to me to cling to the images as Eliot employs them. [f]

---

[f] This source was suggested to me by a student who happened to have been reading Wilde at the time. Dame Helen Gardner records someone else's suggestion to her that the group of images originates with Kipling's story *They* (Gardner, pp. 159-160). That is possible too, though the spirit and the imagery of Wilde's story are closer to those of Eliot.

In his notes to the French translation of the *Four Quartets (Quatre Quatuors*, Paris: Editions du Seuil [1950] p. 155) John Hayward described the cluster of images as a reminiscence, general but not particular, by Eliot of his childhood. As they appear in the poems, however, the images seem to me rather the grown-up's view of the child's world, not a recovered sense of what that world felt like to the child—not, for example, like the reality in which chair legs and table legs loom as an important part of life (as in *Animula*). It is not so much the pleasure and excitement experienced by the children, as it is our own pleasure in hearing their excited laughter. These images also lack both the strong nostalgic coloring

The little "New Hampshire" poem is of interest mainly as one of the none-too-many counterweights to the imagery of Eliot's severer moods. The other "Landscape" that demands notice is a different matter altogether; it stands alone and on its own value. *Rannoch, by Glencoe* is Eliot's only great short lyric; it is also one of the best—and most somber—of modern short lyrics though it has remained half-buried and wholly unnoticed in this group of brief, generally undistinguished descriptive poems. For its full effect, the reader needs a modicum of historical information.

The geographical landscape of *Rannoch* is a high bleak Scottish moor bordering a deep and narrow glen, the scene in 1692 of a treacherous massacre, the bitter memories of which have never been extinguished; nor have its origins been fully exposed though its vaguely known connection with the "pacification" of the Highlands gave it much more than local meaning. As a reviewer of John Prebble's *Glencoe* wrote in the 1960s, the episode "belongs to the category of bloodshed by breach of confidence that is never forgotten." The poem is best read with a general but not a detailed awareness of the event, for histories of the massacre are full of people, alive and dead; whereas the moor of the poem is a solitude.

Eliot usually required space to move about in. *Rannoch, by Glencoe*, however, has all the space in the world, within its twelve lines, for present desolation, past war, and treachery unforgotten and unreconciled. Almost everything is said in the opening stark and concentrated images —here even "the crow starves," and the stag breeds only

---

and the visual precision which—one or both—elsewhere characterizes the imagery deriving from Eliot's earlier memories. If the children, apple-blossoms, birds, laughter are memory at all, they seem memory heavily overlaid by another's imagination, probably Wilde's, from which they take their character and significance, for in Eliot they are marked less by empathy (detestable word but sometimes unavoidable) or recollection than by structural symbolic *intention*.

that the hunter may shoot, in a land as waste as Ezekiel's
or the Waste Land itself. Everything needful is said between the first bitter ellipsis and the close:

Here the crow starves, here the patient stag
Breeds for the rifle. Between the soft moor
And the soft sky, scarcely room
To leap or soar. Substance crumbles, in the thin air
Moon cold or moon hot. The road winds in
Listlessness of ancient war,
Languor of broken steel,
Clamour of confused wrong, apt
In silence. Memory is strong
Beyond the bone. Pride snapped,
Shadow of pride is long, in the long pass
No concurrence of bone.

This is the dark side of unity of culture, the moment
of time none can redeem, a Waste Land contracted into
the single scene of a present indelibly but invisibly marked
by the past. Through grim metaphorical distortions of the
natural world, mere geological infertility and the customary activity of hunter become the external marks of ancient
wrong, a desert antithetical to the beneficent desert of *Ash
Wednesday* where the garden would bloom and time could
be redeemed. In *Rannoch, by Glencoe* the links of time
are unbreakable; there is and will be "no concurrence of
bone." This final line, with its understatement in the
abstraction of "concurrence," gains some part of its resonance from being the specific reversal of those glad com-
plaisant bones that one remembers from *Ash Wednesday*;
it is a line which goes far toward making up for many
of the more contrived patterns of Eliot's repeated imagery
elsewhere. All other allusion submerged, the few lines of
this lyric create a universe of desolation that in spirit
includes the personal with the geographical and historical,
the moral with the cosmic. There is nothing else resembling

it in Eliot: it stands isolated among the later religious poems but does not properly resemble the earlier work either; beside it the gloom of *Gerontion*, and even perhaps of *The Waste Land*, sound a trifle plaintive and that of *The Hollow Men* petty.

I prefer to read *Rannoch, by Glencoe* by and for itself, except for the indirect allusion to the bones of *Ash Wednesday* in the last line, which seems an essential part of the poem. It has, however, its links to other works if one cares to note them: the starving crow and the oppressive closeness of earth and sky both become part of the foreboding atmosphere of *Murder in the Cathedral*; the reflections on history and time we have met in *Gerontion* and elsewhere and will meet again in the Quartets.

Frank Morley records the visit with Eliot to Rannoch Moor in November 1933, shortly after the return from America which marked the final separation of Eliot from his wife. John Buchan had published that year a small book on the Glencoe Massacre. Before his return from America, in his lectures at the University of Virginia, Eliot had described our own Civil War as "a disaster from which the country has never recovered, and perhaps never will: we are always too ready to assume that ... the ill-effects are obliterated by time." Our Civil War and Glencoe together are part of all that is abstracted shortly afterwards in the generalizing of *Burnt Norton*: "If all time is eternally present/ All time is unredeemable." And in the lectures at Virginia he might have been foreseeing the result of the visit he would pay to Rannoch: "Landscape," he said, "is a passive creature which lends itself to an author's mood."[7]

From this time on—from about 1934, that is—the creative energy of Eliot began to move in a new direction. The *Four Quartets* were written; but for the rest, his attention turned to poetic drama for the public theater, and here, except for brief illustration of its relation to the poems,

I do not mean to follow him, primarily because the plays seem to me on the whole inferior both as drama and as poetry. For all his years of pondering the prospect for our time of a viable language, style, and "convention" for poetic drama such as the Elizabethan and Jacobean dramatists had once created (though imperfectly, as he felt, with respect to a "convention") the solution eluded him as it has eluded other modern poets. This I think true despite the respectable success of several of the plays in the public theater and the favorable critical attention which several have received. Eliot's own opinion to the contrary notwithstanding, *Murder in the Cathedral* is the best of them: Eliot makes a kind of Coriolanus out of Becket, a Coriolanus who however does not break but masters his fate through his martyrdom. There is poetry in some of the choruses and pith and eloquence elsewhere.

The plays that followed, though they belong to the world of English social comedy (constructed over a ground base of Greek tragedy), deal with conversion, pride, guilt, renunciation, above all with inner spiritual change, subjects that obviously still engaged Eliot's thought. But whereas the poems had in fact dramatized his theme, the plays as a whole scarcely do; they merely talk about it, in often puerile chitchat. Very likely this chatter was intended to be the "consistent convention" which the Elizabethans had lacked, but the speech is too characterless to function as a formative convention. It is not the flexible colloquial speech of everyday life, nor is it this stylized or transfigured in verse; it is often, in fact, dead. The people are dead too; and as automatons they are not stylish enough to be successful: Sweeney and Doris and Dusty, and their speech with its flat, prancing repetitions had been more stylish. *The Cocktail Party* opens with what is evidently intended as a refinement upon those earlier inanities with their music-hall parrot-patter of echoing half-lines, at a different social level; but the rhythms and the stylization are now so cautious that they scarcely tell: instead of stylish flatness we hear ordinary flatness; and as the play proceeds, lack of tension in the writing continues at war with the seriousness of the theme.

In all these plays the theme of change is still dominant. In *The Cocktail Party*, where it is the whole subject, it is discussed in scene after scene; the characters change— more precisely, are said to change, since one can only take the author's word for this when Celia moves from a parody of cocktail society to a parody of martyrdom, the most arbitrarily gruesome of martyrdoms, crucifixion beside a tropical anthill.

How persistent Eliot was with his old theme and how lifeless was the result, is apparent in a later play, *The Confidential Clerk*:

LUCASTA: I think I'm changing.
                I've changed quite a lot in the last two hours.
COLBY: And I think I'm changing too. But perhaps what we
                                call change . . .
                                [Eliot's periods]
LUCASTA: Is understanding better what one really is.
                And the reason why that comes about perhaps . . .
                                [Eliot's periods]
COLBY: Is, beginning to understand another person.

                                                Act II

And later on:

LUCASTA: Goodbye to Colby as Lucasta knew him,
                And goodbye to the Lucasta whom Colby knew.
                We've changed since then: as you said, we're
                                always changing.

                                                Act III

True enough, one feels, but what then?—Eliot undertook to weave the plays as well as the poems into the unity of his lifetime's work, but that fact and not the dramatic writing itself is all the reader interested primarily in the poetry need attend to.[8] For the student of drama, to be sure, and in terms of Eliot's themes and designs, the problems presented by the plays must be taken more seriously, for essentially they involve the translation of upper-class Sweeneys, Dorises, and Dusties into a Greek drama which should appeal to the wide and miscellaneous audience that Eliot said he desired, or, conversely, the translation of Greek drama into the conventions and language of upper-class Sweeny-Doris-Dusty, stylized: the upshot, moreover, would have to be a Christian morality play centering about a "salvation" character. Few dramatic undertakings could be more difficult, or more interesting to comtemplate, but they are not my present subject.

Four Quartets

There all the barrel-hoops are knit,
There all the serpent-tails are bit,
There all the gyres converge in one,
There all the planets drop in the sun.

Yeats, *There*

* * * * *

At the still point of the turning world.

MUSIC AND POETRY

Four Quartets represents one more, and the last, significant change in the work of Eliot the poet: what he had
now to say is again different, its spirit is different, its
expression must be different. In *Ash Wednesday* and the
best of the Ariel poems he had been transposing into poetry
what in prose he summed up as the "conscious attempt,
as difficult and hard as rebirth, to pass through the
looking-glass into a world which is just as reasonable as

our own" and which may prove "larger and more solid." [a]
Without looking too closely into all he may have meant
or not meant by the image of Alice's looking-glass, we saw
the passage through the glass accomplished; and the Quartets speak from beyond it.

Not immediately however. A time of poetic sterility
following the years of the "conversion" poems had brought
forth only one notable poem, of twelve lines. Eliot seemed
to himself, he said afterwards, "to have exhausted [his]
meagre poetic gifts, and to have nothing more to say."[1]
The stagnation was dispelled only by a commission several
years later to supply verse for *The Rock* in 1934; this had
moved his pen if not all his poetic power to renewed activity.
Murder in the Cathedral followed the next year; and
passages from it, rejected as unsuitable for the stage,
furnished a nucleus around which *Burnt Norton* grew. Five
more years elapsed and the Second World War had begun
before the second Quartet was written; the third and fourth
then followed in successive years during the war.

The new style in which Eliot would speak from his now
established spiritual world had been described prospective-
ly in a lecture of 1933: he wished, he said, to create either
a poetry "with nothing poetic about it, poetry standing
naked in its bare bones, or ... poetry so transparent that
in reading it we are intent on what the poetry *points at*,
and not on the poetry." To accomplish this would be "to
get *beyond poetry*, as Beethoven, in his later works, strove
to get *beyond music*."[2] This passage and the evident
"transparency" alternating with "bare bones" in the style
of the poems to come, together with their pointed title
"Quartets" and Eliot's well-known and enduring admiration for Beethoven's music, all direct us to the musical

[a] The statement (*Selected Essays* p. 276) is made ostensibly with
reference to our reading of Dante but the wider Christian reference is
obviously intended. (Query: Is "difficult *and hard*" an oversight, or has
it meaning?)

inspiration not only of the new styles but also of the new
form, which proves to be, in the distant parallels of verse,
a composite of the late quartets of Beethoven, particularly
the C sharp minor (Opus 131) and the A minor (Opus 132),
probably the Bartók quartets which have been described
as modern developments from the late Beethoven, and—I
am sure Herbert Howarth was right about this—J. W. N.
Sullivan's *Beethoven: His Spiritual Development* (1927);[3]
Sullivan, in fact, not least.

Though the usual string quartet is made up of four
movements, Eliot could have found in several of Bartók's,
as well as in the A minor quartet of Beethoven, a musical
precedent for the form in five movements which he adopted
for the poems. He would have found in the fourth and
fifth quartets of Bartók, also, the linking of separate
movements by recurring and related themes, something
which was only beginning to appear in Beethoven's late
music. Mainly, however, it is Beethoven and Sullivan's
account of Beethoven, that mark the *Four Quartets*. The
musical analogies are not to be pursued too far, as Eliot
warned just before the last of his Quartets appeared: what
he believed music could offer the poet were mainly suggestions for structure and rhythm, possibilities of comparable
transitions, and "possibilities of contrapuntal arrangement
of subject-matter."[4] He needed no musical analogy for the
use of recurrent imagery, but perhaps this too was intensified by his attention to musical structure. Eliot's technical
knowledge of music, he always said, was not extensive, and
very often in the *Four Quartets* what we are aware of is
Sullivan's emphasis, Sullivan's ideas about Beethoven,
Sullivan's verbal interpretation of the music, and occasionally Sullivan's words. I do not mean that Eliot was
insensible to the music itself. But the gap between music
and language is such that few attempts to translate or
paraphrase musical "meaning" succeed; Sullivan probably
does better than most. The opening fugue of the C sharp

minor quartet does not "mean" to me quite what Sullivan puts into words as its meaning, but then I could not attempt to put its meaning into any words whatever, and Sullivan does find words for a conceivable emotional and spiritual "meaning" or at least state of mind. His verbal description of the fugue might be more readily available, more directly suggestive, for a poet's purpose than the music alone could be. It was to a great extent this, I think, that Eliot found himself using.

His choice of a five-part rather than the standard four-part form of the string quartet has raised among critics speculation which leads to other questions, tantalizing to the mind, regarding a whole class of integral but composite art-forms; it is an idle enough interest but momentarily irresistible. From the Aristotelian beginning, middle, and end, through the cosmos of the Divine Comedy and through nearly the whole of drama, down to the Hegelian triad and our body-mind-soul view of ourselves, by means of the three-part or its variant five-part form we have managed to see the universe and ourselves nicely organized on a comprehensible foundation. Two and four won't do. As William Gilpin observed in the eighteenth century, two cows "will hardly combine" in a landscape. If this formula seems to disregard the sexes, no matter. But somehow we did invent the two-part Italian sonnet and then all the great four-part sonata forms in music (quartet, sonata, symphony), and must wonder where these leave our theories of satisfactory form. My serious point is this, that critical speculations on the meaning or rationale of these numerical divisions in Eliot's composite poems do not get very far. *The Waste Land* gave us the five of earth, air, fire, water, and an inclusive finale; the five of *The Hollow Men* may well have been a matter of chance. The six of *Ash Wednesday* nobody that I know of has accounted for; presumably six stages of spiritual progress found objective correlatives that could be brought into a suitable final relationship. The unstandard five-part quartet form might be thought deliberately chosen to echo, somewhat routinely, the parts of *The Waste Land,* or might have been chosen with reference to Christian symbolism, as the form of the Good Friday lyric of *East Coker* evidently was, but since nothing within the poems bears out the latter intention, it is not an operative symbol. What is clear and what most matters about these composite forms of Eliot is that they are never open-ended. The finale of *The Waste Land,* even lacking a definitive answer to the question of the poem, is what all the preceding leads to; *Ash Wednesday,* though its progression is chronologically linear, closes a circular form with its return to the opening lines in Part VI. Each Quartet is self-enclosed by a return of theme or imagery at the end, and the series of the four together create loosely the three-part effect of reflections springing from family and self (II and III) enclosed within a frame of broader reference. The last Quartet encloses all by including as well as answering the first and is, besides, the final recapitulation of a life's journey.

Sullivan has a rationale for the late Beethoven's choice of forms. In the conclusion of his book he reminds the reader that throughout he has regarded Beethoven "chiefly as an explorer": even at the end of a lifetime, ill, deaf, solitary, and in rags, composing the greatest of the late quartets he remained "an explorer" (and we remember being told toward the end of *East Coker* that all "old men ought to be explorers," and at the end of *Little Gidding* and of Eliot's own poetry, that "we shall not cease from exploration"). Music in the usual sonata form of four movements represents a natural psychological progression, Sullivan maintains—separate but ordered "stages in a journey"; this is his explanation of why, by convention, the movements, moods, and tempi follow each other in a prescribed order, together making up the standard four-part form. The order is *linear.* But Beethoven's last and greatest quartets, those in which "Beethoven the explorer is most clearly revealed," are different: the A minor has five, the B flat major six, and the C sharp minor seven movements, not for numerical reasons but because now instead of a linear progression "the movements radiate, as it were," in various directions from a "dominating, central experience" which Sullivan sees as a mystical experience or "mystic vision." The music no longer records "a spiritual history"; it now represents a "vision of life," and the experiences of the other movements are seen in the light of the central one. The supreme achievement is the C sharp minor quartet. It is "the most mystical" of them all and "the one where the mystical vision is most perfectly sustained"; it represents "that serenity which ... passes beyond beauty," a "state of illumination" which can only occur in moments of "profoundest abstraction from the world." The visionary center of this quartet is the great opening fugue[5] (admittedly that fugue is one of the very high points of all chamber music).

Whether or not Sullivan's analysis of Beethoven's "linear" and "radiating" musical form is accepted, and whether his Beethoven is everyone's Beethoven does not matter. His conception of the spirit and form of the C sharp Minor is in itself an intelligible concept; it is also one which could as well grow into a poem as into a string quartet; and I think did. By comparison with the "difficult and hard" rebirth of *Ash Wednesday* and the *Journey of the Magi*, the world beyond the looking-glass of the Quartets is a world of serenity. There are still things to be striven for, still to regret, but they are no longer urgent, for essential change is now past.

Eliot was not a mystic; but through these final poems the *thought* of mystical experience is rarely far off, and something half suggesting a mystical vision appears early in *Burnt Norton*. I myself am not competent to speak of mystical experience, but there is what I take to be a dimmer

but cognate experience known to most of us—that of certain
rare moments during which, sometimes for no identifiable
reason, external pressures drop away; striving and apprehension, anxiety or ambition for the future and grief, guilt,
regret, resentments for the past vanish; and one seems
to exist with happiness, wholly in the present, for brief
moments only. This I think of as the psychological version
of the religious experience—without its making any claim,
however, to the significance of moments felt and believed
to be union with the Divine. Yeats described the experience
in *Per Amica Silentia Lunae* without much belief in its
mystical validity; it came to him at certain times, unforeseen, when hatred, he thought, "the common condition
of our life," melted away for perhaps an hour.[6] The poem
Vacillation (Part IV) describes one of these occasions, and
Demon and Beast opens with an account of another:

> For certain minutes at the least
> That crafty demon and that loud beast
> That plague me day and night
> Ran out of my sight;
> Though I had long perned in the gyre,
> Between my hatred and desire,
> I saw my freedom won
> And all laugh in the sun.

The portraits in the gallery all welcome him; outside,
the sight of a mere gull and an "absurd/ Portly green-pated
bird" makes him irrationally happy. Unlike Eliot, however,
he was certain that "mere growing old, that brings/ Chilled
blood, this sweetness brought." Yeats grew notably more,
as Eliot grew less, sceptical with age.

Some such experience, the scene in the rose garden, is
the center of *Burnt Norton*; and from it the other movements "radiate out" in various directions. The experience
is described again briefly, in more abstract and explicit
terms, in the second movement of *The Dry Salvages*:

The moments of happiness—not the sense of well-being,
Fruition, fulfilment, security or affection,
Or even a very good dinner, but the sudden illumination—
We had the experience but missed the meaning,
And approach to the meaning restores the experience
In a different form, beyond any meaning
We can assign to happiness.

BURNT NORTON

Burnt Norton the place is a manor in the Cotswolds the grounds of which Eliot visited while staying in the neighborhood in 1934. Unlike the scenes of the other place-named Quartets, it had no particular associations for him; these were merely the empty gardens of an estate with trees, a pleached alley or one bordered by trees or shrubbery, boxwood-bordered walks, [b] a rose-garden, a drained concrete lily pool. There were other features too, but these are the materials of Eliot's opening scene.

The poem begins with abstractions, the statement of a theme in measured accentual verse (but not the earlier drumbeats) of four stresses: [c]

[b] An irrelevancy here should be got rid of, if possible:
      we moved ... in a formal pattern,
      Along the empty alley, into the box circle—

i.e., entered the box circle of the theater through a back door in the alley: so more than one urban reader who has had neither experience nor dream of a formal garden. This is a pity because it destroys the mood; it will not in any way do in the context even as an Empsonian ambiguity: in the back alley one does not move in a "formal pattern," for one thing, but that is the least of the objections.

[c] Four-Stress lines, though they are not its only rhythm, dominate the whole of *Burnt Norton* but with remarkable variety of effect in the different movements. For detailed discussion of the rhythms, see Helen Gardner's opening chapter and the unpublished dissertation of Lynn Hamilton, "The Auditory Imagination: T. S. Eliot" (University of California, Santa Barbara, 1973). To me the rhythm does not sound as if it sprang (as parts of *Murder in the Cathedral* certainly did) from the Anglo-Saxon or from *Piers Plowman* as Dame Helen seems to imply, but she is aware of the differences, and the question of origin is not very material.

Time present and time past
Are both perhaps present in time future,
And time future contained in time past.
If all time is eternally present
All time is unredeemable.

The unbreakable linkage of time is accepted, and there is no doom about it here as there had been in *Rannoch*; still, there is speculation: supposing one had made the other choice, the choice that remains always a possibility when regarded speculatively. In a further sense, what might have been is even a part of what is, all the possibilities of the past being part of the present by virtue of having existed as possibility. It is a formulation of thought not unlike Keats's statement that what the mind seizes as beauty must be truth, "whether it existed before or not." Hence,

What might have been and what has been
Point to one end, which is always present.

Well, this is what Eliot had said he wanted, all right, the "bare bones of poetry." But it states a theme from which the question is posed: is there any way of breaking, of transcending, these unbreakable links of time? Ultimately the poem is about those seemingly timeless moments that do "redeem" time spiritually if not historically. The single-voiced abstract bones of the opening are quickly made concrete, and the unadorned theme which might have been the opening statement of the C sharp minor fugue gathers other voices or echoes. [d] We hear the footfall of memory

[d] As was implied earlier, musical parallels are more nearly metaphor than close analogy. In any literal sense, counterpoint in language would require that different speakers utter different sentences simultaneously. Simultaneous layers of *meaning*, however, may be readily felt as contrapuntal when handled in certain ways. Dame Helen Gardner finds sonata-form in Eliot's first movement. I think of it rather as fugue-like; but the parallels in either case are so figurative that one might conceivably hear it as either. It is the single-voiced opening followed by the many-layered, many-voiced scene that suggests to me an intended fugal structure; and the awareness of fugal form makes more vividly present to me this many-voiced character of the first movement.

echoing down the corridor of the choice we did not take into the rose-garden we might have entered: "we," "I," "you," each his own footfalls, moving differently but together.

The pattern is complicated: for there is the rose garden of the past which the poet did not enter but might have entered, and the actual rose garden of Burnt Norton which he now enters, and the rose garden which is the mystical timeless moment or the nonmystical sense of pure Now which contains the past but is free of its "enchainments." And there is, further, the rose bowl, holding last year's rose petals spiced and still fragrant with the memory of last summer's roses. [e] As memory, the bowl is dusty; later in the poem without dust it is art, which itself represents the timeless Now that holds the past. The scene as represented in the poem reads to me as though the actual visit of Eliot had perhaps been the occasion of one of those timeless moments, not a true mystical experience, which one gathers Eliot never had, but one similar to Yeats's releases from "hatred and desire," anxiety, guilt, or what-

[e] The rose bowl, like the alley and the box circle, I have known to trail clouds of a different glory, transformed by capitalization and memories of football; this too is a destructive ambiguity that can only make an irrelevant joke of the context. If Possum had it in mind, as a friend (of mine, not Eliot's) has suggested to me, he should not have had it. Nor is the bowl in the poem, as other readers have supposed, a vase for fresh flowers. The symbol would have presented neither of these ambiguities to a reader of Eliot's generation or background. My own paternal grandmother had a rose bowl, Chinese, decorated with a scroll design, and topped with a double lid and stopper which was opened to perfume the air of the parlor faintly with last summer's dried and spiced rose petals, on Sunday afternoons when friends called or on weekday afternoons when the minister came for tea. It was called a rose bowl (not a *pot pourri*) and was not then at all unusual in an old-fashioned sitting room or parlor. (I know of one such bowl still in use that came from Eliot's native city St. Louis.) In the poem it is an important and natural symbol for the fragrant past, the past first as memory, afterwards as art. (For some readers this gloss will undoubtedly be superfluous, but to many, even sophisticated, modern readers the grotesque or simply colorless associations have been destructive to the tone and sense of the poem.)

ever else chains us to time past and time future. Either
Eliot had that experience at the time or, knowing it from
other occasions, chose now to place it here in the garden,
where it is blended with the imagined innocence (innocence,
too, is without past or future) of "our first world," both
childhood and Eden, partly a garden we knew but mainly
one we "might have" entered. It is thus full of "echoes"
of the past—mankind's, our individual own, those of the
unknown former dwellers in Burnt Norton, all the "Other
echoes." All the "they's" are echoes and all the echoes
are welcome: this is "our" moment now, "they" are "our
guests." The eyes once a source of torment are not seen
but are present and welcome too, and this feeling is
projected upon the roses which are pleased to be looked
at. We and "they," the echoes, move through the green
alley and the boxwood circle to the dry pool, now by illusion
of sunlight filled with water, with lotus blossom, with
reflections of the presences behind us, and we hear the
hidden laughter of children in the leaves for the moment
of blessed happiness. But the timeless moment, in which
neither past nor future is a threat or a burden, cannot
last, the cloud covers the sun, the pool is empty, and we
are back within the links of time.

Was the experience real or illusion? The answer of course
is that it was both, for the scene is framed by the voice
of the thrush, the "deception" of whose invitation to enter
we had followed; but we are sent away in the end because,
its voice tells us, "human kind/ Cannot bear very much
reality." And the scene is further framed by repetition of
the lines that precede the first footfalls: both the *might
have been* and the *has been* are always present; hence
the scene has been both illusion and reality: the experience
has been a true symbol, a type, of a mystical vision though
not the actually experienced direct communion with the
Divine.

With all its complexity, there is a "transparence" about

the scene, if one may use that word without being asked what is beyond the transparence. It is, at any rate, Eliot's almost visionary C sharp minor fugue, like the fugue structurally complex, saying many things at once, yet serene in spirit (this is not to compare Eliot's stature with Beethoven's; I speak only of the structure and the mood, and of the mood only as Sullivan describes it); from this scene the later movements of the quartet "radiate out" in meditative, expository, and lyrical explorations of its meanings, analogues, and implications. In style, the suc- ceeding movements range from even greater "transpar- ence" to barer bones. In structure, substance, and succes- sion of moods they go their own way, however: *Burnt Norton* as a whole is not strictly modeled upon any one quartet by Beethoven, or Bartók. [f]

The transparent opening lyric of the second movement is Eliot's recantation of *The Waste Land*'s fear of spring, and it is also the poet's elation, distantly corresponding to Beethoven's hymn of thanks for recovery from illness, his "Heiliger Dankgesang an die Gottheit eines Genesenen, in der lidischen Tonart" ("Sacred song of thanks to the Godhead from one recovered [from illness], in the Lydian mode"), particularly the part marked by Beethoven "Neue Kraft fühlend" and described by Sullivan as the "quickened life, a rush of celestial joy."[7] With the completion of *Murder in the Cathedral* and the plan and execution of a new kind of poem well advanced, Eliot's exhausted and sterile

---

[f] Howarth's discovery of the influence of Sullivan on Eliot's *Quartets* is illuminating, but I think Howarth errs in trying to force the poems into a continuing parallel, not with the C sharp minor but with the A minor quartet of Beethoven. The A minor's five movements and some of their tempi may have influenced Eliot, and its "Heiliger Dankgesang" I feel sure did; but there is no similarity in Eliot to the mood of that quartet as a whole. Sullivan describes it as expressing the depths of human pain and spiritual weariness. The A minor is not quite that to me, but neither is its mood in general comparable to that of *Burnt Norton* or Eliot's other Quartets.

period had truly ended; he was alive again as a poet, and
he says so in this singing lyric with, as in the preceding
movement, the richest possible texture of associations. One
of the two epigraphs of *Burnt Norton* is "The way up and
the way down are the same," and this movement is the
Heraclitean ascent, beginning in the mud and ending
among the stars.

> Garlic and sapphires in the mud
> Clot the bedded axle-tree.
> The trilling wire in the blood
> Sings below inveterate scars
> Appeasing long forgotten wars. [g]
> The dance along the artery
> The circulation of the lymph
> Are figured in the drift of stars
> Ascend to summer in the tree.

The lines have been incompletely and sometimes misleadingly glossed. Their opening image originated, no
doubt, as Eliot said, with the line of Mallarmé, "Tonnerre
et rubis aux moyeux," "Thunder and rubies at the hubs,"
following an ironic line in which Mallarmé says he is
"joyeux" though he was not. Eliot, however, was maintain-
ing a stronger hold than Mallarmé on the literal. Everybody knows sapphire skies and emerald grass, which of
course a self-respecting poet does not now mention. [h] But
spring in the country or on the fringes and in the unpaved
byways of town used to mean—in Cambridge (Mass.) or
elsewhere—deep mud from the spring thaw, miring a wagon
or car up to its axletree; puddles reflecting blue sky; and

---

[g] A late revision of the earlier line, "And reconciles forgotten wars,"
which to this reader seems superior in spite of a second "reconcile" in
the last line. The original line was retained as late as 1952.

[h] Cf., however, even the relatively modern John Davidson's lines in
The Testament of a Prime Minister, of "green and sapphire earth," with
"Crystal snow" at its poles and "sumptuous rubies" at its middle.

garlic—just common wild garlic or onion, the earliest spring green along roadside or in pasture, and the earliest spring weed to rise up in the brown lawn. In damp woods or swamps skunk cabbage comes first, but Eliot knew where to draw the line. Or did he? Though natural to the spring scene, garlic may possibly have been chosen partly by Eliot-*Possum* and may be to that extent a blemish, being, if one misses the natural spring image, out of phase with the prevailing mood. *Axle-tree* is anyhow a fine word (a pity we now usually say merely *axle*, ignoring the cross-bar): here it carries its legendary and cosmic associations as in Chapman but carries them lightly, for the word is bedded in common use—brightened, though, for one who has recently read Sullivan, by Beethoven's wonderful image of its sound in breaking. He had just written what proved to be his last completed work (the F major quartet), while staying briefly at a place called Gneixendorf: "The name sounds like the breaking of an axle-tree," Sullivan quotes him as writing in a letter.[8]

"The trilling wire in the blood" that "sings" as the violins sing, "the dance along the artery," "the circulation of the lymph," all part of the ascending motion—this is recovery from illness in blood, artery, lymph; and it is the now unreluctant revival of life in spring. The past, though it cannot be quite undone, is healed into mere "scars," and past wars are both reconciled and forgotten (the bones of Glencoe already forgotten). In this elation one soars with the violins above the trees, above the old patterns of earth, the patterns of pursuer and pursued, which now like the wars are reconciled among the constellations. The lyric is a parable of recovery of creative power and the elation that goes with it. If it is really listened to, its lightness (the smooth regular iambics, with one of its four stresses almost invariably lightened), the spirit of its *Erhebung* will be quickly felt. Eliot used the German word in the prosaic passage that follows, I imagine, because, at least to a foreign ear, it seems to carry more of its pure literal sense of "lifting up" and fewer other connotations than such possible English equivalents as *exaltation* or *elevation.*

The ascending movement of this lyric of Part II is balanced by descending movement at the close of Part III. Life-giving though both are, neither represents the ultimate spiritual experience; and so between the ascent and the descent stands the expository prosaic sequel to the lyric, defining what that experience truly is, and the opening of Part III, which presents what it most is not. The ultimate experience is "the still point of the turning world." It is "neither ascent nor decline," even its *Erhebung* is "without motion": it is the timeless moment in which the chains of past and future are loosed, in short, the true mystical experience, of which the not quite mystical moment in the garden is a hint. We can experience the moment briefly but can retain it only by bringing it back with us through memory into time (as Eliot had suggested several years earlier, writing of Pascal's mystical experience), where it can still cast its radiance over our daily "time":

> only in time can the moment in the rose-garden,
> The moment in the arbour where the rain beat,
> The moment in the draughty church at smokefall
> Be remembered; involved with past and future.
> Only through time time is conquered.

Let us not "interpret" the moment in the draughty church at smokefall: "There is a logic of the imagination as well as a logic of concepts,"[9] and this is it; we have all been there. In the arbour where the rain beat also.

Part III juxtaposes two opposite kinds of darkness and descent, the first that aspect of daily life and that class of persons at the farthest remove from the timeless rose-garden, the "men and bits of paper," men with "strained time-ridden faces" in the London Tube with its "dim light" and the characteristic stale chilling draught of under-ground systems, men in perpetual purposeless movement from one to another of the "gloomy hills of London." This is the world of Dante's dead souls who crossed London Bridge in *The Waste Land*, and it is also the "twittering" world of the shades, Homer's dead. But against this descent is set the other, that of St. John of the Cross, for whom, as for Heraclitus, the way up and the way down are the same. The recovered self that "ascends to summer" in the second movement is balanced now by the soul's descent: the ascent has seemed to imply the rebirth of poetic creativity, the descent, spiritual renewal.

The fourth movement, a short lyric as it is in all the Quartets, refers us back to the garden. We are not in it, however, either in illusion or in reality. Our experience in the garden had been momentary, ending as the "cloud passed, and the pool was empty." Now this is taken up again—the "cloud carries the sun away"—and the question is asked: shall we ever really possess the garden? The images are all of what we were not shown before, sunflower, clematis, yew. But we ask more: will the garden be *ours*—real for us, not illusive vision? "Will the súnflower túrn to ús, will the clematis ... bend to us?" For the answer we are told only what we knew: the rose-garden exists, is still "there," to represent "the still point of the turning world." There is reassurance if not quite a promise.

The final movement brings this all down, first directly to the world of the artist, the artist in music as well as in words, and in terms that remind the reader again here and there of Sullivan's discussions of the artist's medium.[i]

---

[i] Sullivan has a great deal to say about the differences between what language and music can express, about Beethoven's hopeless attempts to express himself in words, and about the particular recalcitrance of language as a medium for the expression of the most profound feelings and intuitions, such as those that are expressed musically in the C sharp minor quartet.

Eliot had always conceived the function of the poet broadly; his responsibility was not exclusively aesthetic in a narrow sense, and was not only toward language, to "purify the dialect of the tribe"; earlier it had been as the bearer and constant renewer of tradition. Now poetry and music are conceived as an analogue of the spiritual still point. Their medium—language or musical tone—exists in time; but the essence of art is form and pattern, for through these it is that art and the timeless moment of mystical vision intersect. The work of art gives us the moving world yet the world detached from the claims of before and after. The great quartet, of music or of words, is thus a union of motion and stillness; as the sounds end we experience the whole, beginning and end at once:

> Only by the form, the pattern,
> Can words or music reach
> The stillness, as a Chinese jar still
> Moves perpetually in its stillness.

The motionless rose jar with its constantly moving but unified scroll pattern, holding the rose leaves of the past in a perpetual present, is the figure now of art. It is a perfection to be achieved only with the greatest difficulty. For words are recalcitrant, they "strain,/ *Crack* and sometimes *break*" (do we hear again the breaking "axle-tree" of "Gneixendorf"?). "Shrieking voices ... always assail them" as the poet tries to set them in order.

An immediate turn from these "words" to "the Word" introduces the most baffling passage in *Burnt Norton*. The lines are beautiful, they sound as if they surely mean something distinct and something important for the poem, as if they have a conceptual as well as an emotional meaning. Yet no reading that I know or can think of seems wholly satisfactory.

> The Word in the desert
> Is most attacked by voices of temptation,
> The crying shadow in the funeral dance,
> The loud lament of the disconsolate chimera.

The first difficulty that assails me is what, if we read the first dozen words in the obvious way, must appear presumptuous in the apparent turn from the poet's own struggle with words to the temptation of Christ, the Word, in the wilderness; for "the Word in the desert" takes off from the poet's "words" without so much as a break in the line, an incivility not easily overlooked. Moreover, a passage describing the temptation of Christ—or of St. Anthony either, as has been suggested—injected abruptly at this point in the poem is, as far as I am able to see, an utter irrelevancy. And so I cannot read it in this way. With some forcing it can be read as an ellipsis, the shift from "words" being not to Christ but to our (or the poet's) difficulty, in the midst of our desert, in holding fast to the Word, the temptation then being not Christ's but our own, our hearing of the Word. The sequel makes sense with this reading, and the transition is also possible, without shock, from the poet's struggle with language to his deeper struggle for spiritual perfection (the themes of the spring lyric of Part II and the spiritual "dark night" of III brought together through the shift from words to Word). The voices that tempt *him* are then the crying shadow and the chimera's lament. This reading is not altogether satisfactory either because such an ellipsis is in itself strained, and the unavoidable reminder, in such phrasing, of the other Temptation gives the words still a somewhat presumptuous air. What does seem likely is that Eliot had the two following lines in mind—lines possibly originating in Becket's scene with his Tempters in *Murder in the Cathedral*—and liked them but had difficulty in introducing them here.

They are introduced somehow, at any rate, and what they seem to represent is two kinds of "temptation" which can endanger that recently won serenity from which the whole poem radiates. Both are retrogressive temptations: the first that of becoming again the crying shadow who refuses after all fully and serenely to accept "time present" because of its weight of time past—cannot accept the funeral dance that all time present, all life, is (even Sweeney knew that "death is life and life is death"); the second, not very different, is probably the temptation of self-hatred, arising from guilt. For this "loud lament of the disconsolate chimera" we may have the key in Sir John Davies's *Nosce Teipsum*, which had been the subject of Eliot's essay of 1926 on Davies. Among the countless descendants of the original Chimera is the "Lady" in Davies's little allegory of the sinful soul who, metamorphosed for her sins into a cow, sees her new reflection in a stream and is horrified; in this state,

> Man's soule
> Doth of all sights her owne sight least endure:
> For even at first reflection she espies,
> Such strange chimeraes, and such monsters there,
> . . . .
> As she retires, and shrinkes for shame and feare. [j]

If one does not too much mind this large importation of a context, Eliot's lines may be seen to have what one has always felt they had, an exact, not a vague, equivalence

---

[j] *Nosce Teipsum*, "Of Humane Knowledge," Stanzas 28-32. Besides Davies, the sources usually cited are the biblical accounts of Christ's Temptations, those of St. Anthony of Egypt, and most particularly Flaubert's version of the latter. Among the monstrous creatures in Flaubert's final chapter is a Chimera. Though very likely she (or "he" in Flaubert's early version) was in Eliot's mind as an image, she throws no light on his meaning: barking, yelping, and cavorting restlessly, she is not a figure of happiness but neither is she "disconsolate"; and nothing of Flaubert's symbolism seems referable to *Burnt Norton*. My impression

to a conceptual meaning. (A better reading would still be welcome, however.)

The more generalized conclusion follows: "The detail of the pattern is movement." For the poet and for the symbol of art these words had been true, now for the Christian they are true, "As in the figure of the ten stairs," the figure of St. John of the Cross for the soul's necessary ascending and descending before the final revelation is possible. The abstract expository reflection that follows on stillness and motion, time and the timeless, is terminated by a glimpse that circles back to the opening scene of the rose-garden. Now it is not ambiguous: we know the experience is real—momentary, yet symbolizing the center of all spiritual value in life. And so the question of the fourth movement is answered in the affirmative; the garden *is* for us, is a revelation of truth: "I have seen these things in a shaft of sunlight," the opening chorus in *Murder in the Cathedral* affirms, and *Burnt Norton* concludes:

> Sudden in a shaft of sunlight
> Even while the dust moves
> There rises the hidden laughter
> Of children in the foliage
> Quick now, here, now, always—
> Ridiculous the waste sad time
> Stretching before and after.

The poet has not come to know this reality through immediate intuitive apprehension, not through a directly experienced full mystical union with the Divine; but

---

that Eliot had in mind the episode of Davies (reinforced by the greater prominence of the figure in Flaubert) is strengthened by the auditory and syntactic resemblance between the opening line of Davies' allegory, "As in the fable of the Lady Faire," and Eliot's line, the next but one after "chimera," "As in the figure of the ten stairs." John Hayward, however, who was seeing much of Eliot at the time, in his notes to the French translation of the Quartets refers the reader to the Gospel of St. John and to Flaubert's St. Anthony (but St. John is the one Gospel that does not describe the temptation of Christ).

through the meditative explorations that have radiated out from the timeless moments in the rose garden he has come to know that experience as a type and contingent promise of the real for which one may strive: he has had a glimpse.

EAST COKER

Some five years after writing *Burnt Norton*, Eliot projected the Quartets as a series of four; k and it seems to have been at this time also that he decided to repeat, from *The Waste Land*, the scheme of the Heraclitean elements. *Burnt Norton*, even if after the fact, adequately represents air, with its visionary scene full of echoes and invisible presences; *East Coker* is earth, the ancestral soil from which the poet is sprung. The symbolism is peripheral and somewhat arbitrary but grows in importance in the last two poems, water being central to the scene and imagery of *The Dry Salvages*, and fire to the scene and symbolic meaning of *Little Gidding*.

Burnt Norton served as a pattern for the other Quartets, each a stage further removed from musical parallels but all abounding in the more traditionally "musical" elements of poetry, elaborate interlaced alliteration and assonance. They also contain, as a matter of course now, countless links of phrase, image, and theme with earlier poems and with each other, yet they are for the most part simpler and less obscure than *Burnt Norton*.

k Reports have circulated that the *Four Quartets* were planned from the outset, but in 1953 Eliot said it had been "only in writing '*East Coker*' that [he] began to see the Quartets as a set of four" (an interview reprinted in Bernard Bergonzi, ed., *T. S. Eliot: Four Quartets, A Casebook*, London: Macmillan, 1969, p. 23). In itself *Burnt Norton* does not raise the expectation of a sequel.

Disputes have arisen also over whether we should call the four one poem or a sequence. Some critics adhere conscientiously to the pronoun "it"; but I notice that Eliot himself, evidently without reflection, in the *Paris Interviews* says "they" (pp. 101, 105). For what the opinion is worth, "they" seem to me an inter-related sequence rather than one poem.

East Coker is on the whole inferior to its predecessor, more contrived in execution and cramped by a too rigid adherence to the form previously set. And there are other weaknesses.

Named for the Somerset village from which the New England Eliots had emigrated, *East Coker* is concerned with the poet's English self and English origins. What might have been its epigraph is embedded in its last line and reversed in its first, a translation of Mary Queen of Scots' French motto, "In my end is my beginning," another variant, when doubled back, of the Heraclitean motto Eliot had used for *Burnt Norton*. The first movement opens with reflections on time, as *Burnt Norton* had done, but here it is the decay of houses in time; and the lines are haunted by miscellaneous echoes of others' writing, of Virginia Woolf's prose-poetry on the decay of a house in *To the Lighthouse,* of *The Waves*, of Hopkins's "flesh and fleece, fur and feather" and Edith Sitwell's *Madam Mouse Trots*, and no doubt much else. Like *Burnt Norton* too, these lines are followed by a scene, imaginary but not this time visionary, of what "might have been," the sixteenth-century Eliots and their neighbors from the now crumbled houses circling in the village dance—all described by quotation from Sir Thomas Elyot's *The Boke Named the Governour*. It is widely agreed that the archaism does not come off very well poetically.

The lyric of the second movement, describing autumn in forced terms of the spring, summer, and constellations that had made up the corresponding passage in *Burnt Norton*, is inferior to the earlier lyric, and Eliot may be saying so in the comment that follows—

That was a way of putting it—not very satisfactory:
A periphrastic study in a worn-out poetical fashion—

before proceeding to translate the lyric into prose reflections on the autumn of life (he was now fifty-two). Age, he declares, has not quite the serenity or the ripe wisdom derived from past experience that one had hoped for.[1] The movement ends with a snatch of elegy on the houses and the dancers that his imagination had conjured up in the beginning, a farewell framed in words which blend Vaughan's line "They are all gone into the world of light" with the least perishable lines Robert Louis Stevenson ever wrote:

> Home is the sailor, home from the sea,
>   And the hunter home from the hill.

And so the second movement closes:

> The houses are all gone under the sea.
> The dancers are all gone under the hill.

The third movement opens with a line joining these words to others from *Samson Agonistes*, "O dark dark dark. They all go into the dark," and reflects—again like *Burnt Norton*—the two kinds of darkness in a passage leading to some ten lines of what have become by this time Eliot's rather mechanically constructed paradoxes:

> And what you own is what you do not own
> And where you are is where you are not.

Two lines of this may be effective, ten become mannerism.

East Coker was written for Good Friday, and the fourth movement tells us so in a lyric made up of five five-line stanzas, the form itself being thus an emblem of the wounds of the Crucifixion. In the lyric, Christ is presented as both victim and savior in the figure of the "wounded surgeon" who heals; the earth then is our "hospital/ Endowed by the ruined millionaire" Adam.[10] We may hope to be purified

---

[1] I fancy Eliot had been rereading Robert Bridges, one or two of whose poems keep coming to mind as I read this movement. See especially the close of Bridges's *November* and the lines about old age in *Poor Poll*. Though Eliot was no great admirer of Bridges.

in Purgatory, where "the flame is roses" (this time no doubt the symbolic five-petaled single rose) and the smoke "briars," the Crown of Thorns.

Both in symbolism and in form this Good Friday lyric is rigidly laid out; its poetical effect is rather that of a corpse in a strait jacket—a dutiful, so it seems to this reader, more than a felt tribute. It is also an intrusion, being insufficiently related to the other movements; and Eliot's acknowledged spiritual values seem turned upside down by its not having been made structurally or thematically central to the whole poem and not, on the other hand, by infusion of spirit made part of the daily Christian life in the poem. Altogether, it is in a key too different to be absorbed into the general texture. Even technically, musically, this Good Friday lyric is unsatisfactory. Its stanza opens with three conventional octosyllabic lines followed by a fourth extended to a pentameter and the fifth, further, to a hexameter. The subtle preparation and rhythmic adjustment requisite for this kind of extension, of which Spenser and scarcely any poet since has been master, is absent in Eliot's lyric; all the stanzas limp. In the first, we are apt in reading to crowd all the lines into the four-stress pattern, which is possible if awkward; but afterwards it is impossible, we are at sea, and the rhythm falls apart.

The fifth movement is again in two parts, the first a reflection turned back upon the ever-changing technical problems that a poet faces as his own intentions change: "one has only learnt to get the better of words/ For the thing one no longer has to say," yet one must continue to try. Its concluding section is a kind of musical enlargement or extension of this as the poet reflects now on the changing pattern of all life, but does so in language that recalls his own past work, telescoping echoes that range from the timeless moment of *Burnt Norton* to Prufrock's lamplight and Pipit's photograph album. "Old men ought

to be explorers," he says, having before him for encouragement not only Sullivan's Beethoven but Yeats, recently
dead, and Bridges (*The Testament of Beauty* at eighty-
five).[m] All this is framed by its opening, "Home is where
one starts from"—the ancestral home with which the poem
began—and "In my end is my beginning." These closing
words are preceded by three of the most poetic lines in
the poem, lines evoking the solitude of the ocean over which
his people had once "fared forth" and over which he himself
had returned alone:

> Through the dark cold and the empty desolation,
> The wave cry, the wind cry, the vast waters
> Of the petrel and the porpoise.

It is also the ocean of eternity toward which we must move;
and it foreshadows the third Quartet which was to follow
within a year. *East Coker* is best as it closes; for as a
whole the poem is thin, and from time to time it slips
into didacticism.

> You say I am repeating
> Something I have said before. I shall say it again.
> Shall I say it again?

These lines from the third movement are an explicit defence
of the poem, but the lines themselves read like caricature.[11]

THE DRY SALVAGES

It was long customary to think of Eliot as a poet of
modern urban life, and this is what he obviously was
determined to be in his early Laforguian years. It is also
said that he cared nothing for nature, and it is undeniable
that he settled in London from choice. But there is over-
simplification in the conclusion. Our type figure for the

---

[m] Eliot's forthcoming commemorative lecture on Yeats dwelt chiefly
on his continuing poetic development in old age.

nature poet is Wordsworth, who to live satisfactorily must live in the country, must walk daily alone or with Dorothy, must contemplate and record, often promptly, the current daisy or shepherd boy or spring lamb (an obviously unfair exaggeration). This is the extreme type. Yeats, like Eliot, was reported as indifferent to nature, by friends who had walked out with him in animated and oblivious conversation. That a man does not stop conversation, however, while his soul expands in the presence of daisy or sunset means little, or at least less than we are apt to suppose.

Eliot's poetry, from *The Waste Land* on, contains much natural imagery, some of it literary or traditional in origin or primarily so, but visually imagined as well as symbolic. His literal desert is Ezekiel's and only symbolically his own, his rose grew rather in tradition than on a bush; and others of his images are universalized and probably not always anchored in experience—*The Waste Land*'s dead tree is not Wordsworth's "of many, one," and its cricket may correspond to a feeling rather than a memory. But there is still a large residue of natural imagery, which we meet, often, in the passages most highly charged with emotion, imagery that is clearly his own, remembered. For many people (and, I presume, for poets) nature may be something the eye takes in while the mind is elsewhere; and it is often a familiar, repeated, remembered experience around which associations gradually cluster. The lines concluding *East Coker*, those ending with "the vast waters of the petrel and the porpoise," are a distillation—lines made real by experience repeated, familiar and half-forgotten time after time. Even in the town poetry of the *Prufrock* days there had been an occasional sensuous natural image. I spoke earlier of a small detail, "the bent goldenrod" near the end of *Ash Wednesday*: small though it is, it carries notice of the beginning of the end of summer, of all one's past summers, the "lost" world of what might have been and what has been.

All this is prefatory to saying that *The Dry Salvages* is a very mixed performance. Once before, Eliot had tried to create poetry out of his American past, the past of place, not of individual persons. His early version of "Death by Water," for all its inconsistencies of style and its pseudo-Conrad shipwreck, had been strongly colored by feeling. For *The Dry Salvages* he returned to the Massachusetts coast at Cape Ann, and again nostalgic emotion pervades the imagery and the language. The themes of the Quartets offered him now a symbolic instead of a narrative frame, and at the same time he apparently undertook to half recreate a past self through a method resembling one employed by Virginia Woolf, who had undertaken in *Jacob's Room* to present Jacob mainly by indirection, through the space he occupied in life, his "room," his surroundings. Jacob may be present, but others are talking; or he is not far off while his mother sits by the sea and cries over a letter; or we are shown places Jacob has just left, a toy pail he has forgotten in the rain, shoes he has worn. Though *The Dry Salvages* is not this alone, something very like it is suggested by Eliot's approach in many of the best passages of the poem, not only to the natural remembered scene but indirectly to the poet's past self also, as when the sea

                            tosses
Its hints of earlier and other creation:
The starfish, the horseshoe crab, the whale's backbone;
The pools where it offers to our curiosity
The more delicate algae and the sea anemone.
. . . .
The shattered lobsterpot, the broken oar
And the gear of foreign dead men.

The boy or youth who had known that shore is in these lines; and in others describing the sound of the bell buoy through the fog which

Measures time not our time, rung by the unhurried
Ground swell, a time
Older than the time of chronometers.

Nevertheless, the material of *The Dry Salvages* and the use or uses to which Eliot wished to put it again presented a problem he was unable fully to solve. The effect is one of unresolved conflict between feeling and will: sea, shore, and the precarious human life so immediately subject to the sea still mean to the poet emotionally something other than the Christian symbolism into which they are being fitted. The result is often embarrassing: it is the weakness Eliot himself had ascribed to most writers of devotional verse, that of "writing as they want to feel, rather than as they do feel."[12] The convert's Anglicanism is a shade too conscious and hence too insistent through much of the poem; it has not become the ground of his being while the poem is in progress.

From the beginning, Eliot makes clear that he means to put to symbolic use his reveries over the two scenes chiefly associated with his youth, the Mississippi at St. Louis and the sea at Cape Ann, for in the opening lines the river is represented as "a strong brown god." This is will at work, not imagination; and in the next paragraph we are told that "the river is within us, the sea is all about us." The metaphor has shifted before any use has been made of the brown god. River and sea, time and eternity, motion and motionlessness—hints of these oppositions are perfunctory; it is the actual sea, the Atlantic off Cape Ann, around which the important associations and feelings cluster; and the river virtually disappears from the poem without having served any significant function.

The lyric of the second movement is a modified sestina which, with its impossibly forced lines and rhymes, is even technically inferior to what one expects of Eliot. "We cannot think of a time that is oceanless"—one could

scarcely say this even if the line did *not* have to rhyme
with "motionless"; and the lyric is further marred by its
series of calculated paradoxes—"soundless wailing," emo-
tionless emotion, "unprayable prayer," "movement of pain
that is painless and motionless"—paradoxes frozen into
sheer mannerism or what eighteenth-century Longinians
would have called frigidity. The weakness of all this is
well known (Denis Donoghue calls the rhymes "notorious"),[13] and it is still a mystery that Eliot could have
let the lyric stand.

The third movement begins as reflection but drifts into
the didactic: "Fare forward, travellers!" the poet urges,
by train this time, in parallel with *Burnt Norton*'s spiritually static journey in the London Tube, and then by
ocean liner, upon which he himself had journeyed from
his past to his present. The meaning of these journeys
is defined in terms of his old theme of subjective change:

> Fare forward, you who think that you are voyaging;
> You are not those who saw the harbour
> Receding, or those who will disembark.

But the year is 1941, and the journey of these lines has
a new dimension, for they are framed by Krishna's teaching
on the subject of war, answering Arjuna's scruples about
killing: "You should not grieve for what is unavoidable":
fare forward.[14]

The fourth movement is a lyric of five-line stanzas like
that of *East Coker* but musically much superior as well
as in better keeping with its surroundings:

> Lady, whose shrine stands on the promontory,
> Pray for all those who are in ships, those
> Whose business has to do with fish, and
> Those concerned with every lawful traffic
> And those who conduct them.

The lyric resembles the traditional prayer and hymn for

those at sea, and its tone drops only when the schematic side of Eliot's mind takes charge. "Every lawful traffic" seems written with liturgy in mind, but this prayer has not the excuse, which liturgy may have, of needing to cover every human contingency explicitly. A further lapse occurs near the end in a reminder of the leopards of *Ash Wednesday* and what they reject—with, here, a side glance at Jonah as well. The Lady is asked to pray for those who perish at sea

> in the sea's lips
> Or in the dark throat which will not reject them.

It is hard to imagine what could have induced the poet to write and to retain "the sea's *lips*" or "throat"—gruesome images, visually inexact, out of keeping with the tone. Yet there is beauty elsewhere in the traditional language and spirit of the lyric. At its close the bell buoy, rung by the primordial ground swell, sounds its "perpetual angelus."

The final movement appears designed to fit the poem into the series and to connect it again with earlier themes. It opens with a list, some twelve lines long, of devices by which human beings, whether fishermen's wives in sleepless nights or ourselves, try to read the past and the future; try to evoke the future from horoscope, tea leaves, palmistry; try to "riddle the inevitable," like Madame Sosostris or Doris with cards, "fiddle with pentagrams" (the poet had just completed the second of his symbolic five-line lyrics). We resort to these devices, or to psychoanalysis, or dreams, or drugs; and these will always be with us,

> some of them especially
> When there is distress of nations and perplexity
> Whether on the shores of Asia, or in the Edgware Road.

This is the wartime present, with our futile attempts to escape responsibility or to understand or deal with it. Over against this is set, once again, the timeless moment, which is also the moment both "in and out of time," of which a hint reaches us "in a shaft of sunlight"; the moment whose meaning, only "half guessed," "half understood," is now explicitly the Incarnation:

> Here the impossible union
> Of spheres of existence is actual,
> Here the past and future
> Are conquered, and reconciled.

"For most of us" the experience of the religious mystic will never occur, but we know its truth, the reality of its meaning as it is asserted here, doctrinally.

At every turn in *The Dry Salvages* we come upon what the poem might have been. The passages about the lives of the fishermen and their wives are a more mature expression of feelings we knew in the earlier Eliot: they present a life which he had seen without sharing, blended with feelings of his own, the nostalgia now conveying both imaginative sympathy and the intensified lonely deprivation of one recalling things that others have desired. *The Dry Salvages,* in short, is a greater disappointment than *East Coker* because it is potentially a much finer poem. But once again, for reasons not fully clear, the return in memory to this scene of his early life left his creative tact unsure, and paralyzed his critical judgment in dealing with it. [n]

LITTLE GIDDING

Little Gidding brings into focus all the Quartets but points back most particularly to the first. The center of

[n] For a full-scale attack upon the whole of *The Dry Salvages*, see Donald Davie, "T. S. Eliot: The End of an Era," first published in *Twentieth Century* (1956), and reprinted in both Bergonzi and Kenner's Twentieth Century series collection. Davie sees the faults clearly and finds nothing else. Time may prove him right, though his view of the Quartet as a kind of hodge-podge of parody and Whitman is to me mysterious.

Burnt Norton had been the timeless moment, the moment of full consciousness that comes briefly, unsought and unforeseen, in a place entered by chance. In *Little Gidding* the experience occurs not by gift or chance but is to be won through a pilgrimage: small and obscure, the Anglican shrine of Little Gidding is a place to which one journeys only with purpose, though one may not quite know what one's purpose is or what its result will be. For *Burnt Norton* the symbol is the rose, for *Little Gidding* Pentecostal fire, and in the concluding line of all, "the fire and the rose are one." The end of the spiritual search, then, is to validate in final terms the apparently chance moments of timeless happiness whose meaning at the beginning had been ambiguous.

For the last Quartet Eliot returns to the England of 1942, the third year of this century's greatest war and the three-hundredth anniversary of the opening of England's own Civil War. In time, the two moments of history are counterpointed; and in place, the presently quiet little chapel of the seventeenth-century religious community founded by Nicholas Ferrar, dispersed by the Puritan parliament toward the end of the Civil War, is counterpointed against the London of the German bombers.

Eliot now approached the war of his own day directly for the first time. *East Coker* had been written in its early months, before the disasters ot France and Dunkirk. The uncertainties of Europe and not the poet's middle age only must underlie the disorder of seasons in its "November" lyric—"What is the late November doing/ With the disturbance of the spring"—and the commentary that follows reflecting upon human disorder, the lack of wisdom and the uselessness of our elders' lessons: "We are only undeceived/ Of that which, deceiving, could no longer harm." Gerontion's complaint against the lessons of history comes now with new force. Ours is a region which we traverse with Dante ("per una selva oscura")

in a dark wood, in a bramble,
On the edge of a grimpen,° where is no secure foothold,
And menaced by monsters.

In that Quartet of 1940, however, Eliot had referred to
the war explicitly only once and incidentally, not to say
coolly, when he spoke of his own middle years as a writer,
"twenty years largely wasted, the years of *l'entre deux
guerres—*/ Trying to learn to use words." In *The Dry
Salvages*, though when it was written England had been
through her worst months, the war is still a half-veiled
abstraction. War poetry being even more difficult to write
than good devotional poetry, Eliot was ready to deal with
the subject directly only when he came to *Little Gidding*,
and this was after all the desperate days were past, nearly
two years after the intensive bombing of London had
subsided.

Within the frame chosen for this last poem, the frame
of present war and the war three hundred years past, are
gathered and reconciled the poet's own present and past
and his final affirmation of faith, for himself and for the
world. But many other concerns are gathered up into this
reconciliation. Even history, which before could teach us
nothing, now, though "history may be servitude,/ History
may be freedom," for it too is "a pattern of timeless
moments" in a different sense; "history is now and England" in the "secluded chapel" to which we come to kneel
"where prayer has been valid."

The Heraclitean elements of the series are now complete:
The Dry Salvages had been water, *Little Gidding* is fire.
In the opening scene the imagery corresponding to *Burnt
Norton*'s half real, half visionary garden is the fiery bright-
ness of a winter day, full of the glitter of ice "on pond
and ditch," a blinding glare "in the dark time of the year"

° *Grimpen* has been traced to Conan Doyle, but in fact it needs no
more gloss than do the invented words of Stevens or Lewis Carroll. Within
its context it creates its own grim meaning.

(and the century). "Where is the summer, the unimaginable/ Zero summer?" the poet asks, with a touch of Wallace Stevens in the asking. This midwinter is the season (but "it would be the same" in May or at any time) in which one has come to pray in the remote humble chapel "behind the pig-sty." And it is here that we receive communication not possible from the living but only from the dead whose speech is "tongued with fire"—from history, from the dead of the saintly community, and now from the dead poets from whom the living poet has learned and still can learn.

The second movement opens as in the other Quartets, with a formal lyric, this time one in which a changing refrain recapitulates the Heraclitean formula. Its theme is the destruction from the German bombing, seen as punishment for our spiritual sins:

> Ash on an old man's sleeve
> Is all the ash the burnt roses leave.
> Dust in the air suspended
> Marks the place where a story ended.
> Dust inbreathed was a house—
> The wall, the wainscot and the mouse.
> The death of hope and despair,
>   This is the death of air.

In the last stanza, "Water and fire deride/ The sacrifice that we denied" and "water and fire shall rot" the foundations, which we have neglected, "Of sanctuary and choir./ This is the death of water and fire."

The lyric is followed in this Quartet not, as before, by a prosaic reflective or expository passage but by an extended scene, "imitating," so Eliot said, a canto of the Inferno or Purgatorio, but drawing on his own wartime experience as a fire-watcher—"a hallucinated scene after an air-raid," he called it—composed in an English substitute for Dante's *terza rima*. ᵖ It opens "in the uncertain hour before the

ᵖ In a later talk on "What Dante Means to Me" (reprinted in *To Criticize the Critic*), Eliot explained his technical intention and described

morning,"

> After the dark dove with the flickering tongue
> Had passed below the horizon of his homing

and ends with the "all-clear" signal. Walking his rounds
. on the "dead patrol," he tells us,

> I caught the sudden look of some dead master
> Whom I had known, forgotten, half recalled
> Both one and many.

The world of the living has become so like Purgatory that
the passage between worlds "now presents no hindrance";
and so the "familiar compound ghost" is here, it tells him,

> In streets I never thought I should revisit
> When I left my body on a distant shore.

"I assumed a double part," the poet says of his dialogue,
making clear that the scene is to be taken as invention,
a fiction, not a transcendent "given" vision, no timeless
moment.

> So I assumed a double part, and cried
> And heard another's voice cry: 'What! are *you* here?'
> Although we were not. I was still the same,
> Knowing myself yet being someone other—
> And he a face still forming; yet the words sufficed
> To compel the recognition they preceded.
> And so, compliant to the common wind,
> Too strange to each other for misunderstanding,
> . . . .
> We trod the pavement in a dead patrol.

Between the crisply conjured "Stetson!" in the ships at
Mylae of twenty years earlier and this cloudy compound
revenant, this "face still forming," stands, one feels sure,

---

his difficulties. This cost him, he said, "far more time and trouble and
vexation than any passage of the same length that I have ever written"
(pp. 128-129).

the Idea of Order forming itself from the sea into song at Key West, though Stevens was not one of the "masters," dead or otherwise, to whom the poet Eliot would be likely to pay explicit tribute. The self-created ghost talks to him of the poet's function and the terrible difficulties of his calling, and then, with irony, of its rewards, which are all bitter.

The compound ghost has been variously identified. One writer knows for a fact that it is T. E. Hulme, another with equal certainty that it is Yeats. There is reason to name Mallarmé; Pound and Valéry have been thought of, though as these two were still living some manipulation of the body on a distant shore is required; and Dante, though the sense is strained if he "*re*-visits" London; or Milton, dead but not on a distant shore, or Virgil. The question of identity is somewhat academic, though since the passage seems meant as both tribute and acknowledgement it would be nice to know who is being honored: the conflicting external testimony leaves us with the text and the probabilities.

The poet's insistence on "both one and many" in the "compound" ghost should assure us that at least on its periphery this wraith is widely inclusive; but in substance it appears to be mainly a double tribute to Hulme and Yeats. Hulme was long since dead in the other great war of the century, on a "distant shore," half forgotten and "half recalled" now, but during the crucial years of Eliot's conversion he had been a "master" to whose "thought and theory" Eliot had owed a good deal. The debts were probably in the main to him. But the ghost's bitter reflections on age must derive from Yeats, who had never in any sense been one of the "masters" of Eliot, not even in later years when Eliot wished to explain and atone for his earlier critical misjudgment. The posthumous tribute now was made possible by genuine admiration for the courage and self-knowledge of Yeats's old age. And so the

summoning of the ghost at the beginning of the scene,
made possible by the nearness of the two worlds of living
and dead, and the symbol of the dancer in refining fire
at the close are a specific reminiscence of the beginning
and end of *Byzantium*; the "conscious impotence of rage
at human folly" is Yeats's, and his is the "re-enactment/
Of all that you have done, and been," in *The Circus
Animals' Desertion*. Yeats and Hulme must be the main
figures, though Mallarmé is represented by the ghost's use
of his words, "To purify the dialect of the tribe."

Separate, specific restitution is made to Milton in the
third movement of the Quartet, with the return in thought
from the scene of present war to the Civil War when the
"king at nightfall" three hundred years before had visited
Little Gidding, when "three men, and more" had died on
the scaffold and "one," Milton, "died blind and quiet." The
theme, as this movement opens, is "detachment"—detachment from self, things, persons: it does not mean less of
love, the poet asserts, but an expansion of love "beyond
desire" and hence "liberation/ From the future as well
as the past." Yet it involves acceptance with equanimity,
or more than equanimity, even of the existence of suffering
and sin—of the world's suffering in present war, 1942, as
well as of the old conflict of King and Parliament. The
words affirming serene faith with serene acceptance of sin
are quoted from Lady Julian of Norwich, who has sometimes been described as the greatest of English mystics:

> Sin is Behovely, but
> All shall be well, and
> All manner of thing shall be well.

In this spirit England's past conflicts are looked upon as
reconciled and forgiven. The tone of this whole passage,
however, seems to me a trifle hollow, not only because
of its fourteenth-century archaism but also, and more
particularly, because the asserted serenity comes too easily.

The earlier serenity of *Burnt Norton*, speaking for the self
more than for the world, seems more genuinely felt.

After a short lyrical return of the "dove"—the bombers
with their double fire of war and Pentecost—the fifth
movement opens to recapitulate and reconcile not the
themes of *Little Gidding* only. It is Eliot's farewell to
poetry in the form of an elaborate, rather contrived piece
of contrapuntal music, a complex weaving of images and
phrases from all the Quartets and from earlier poems. The
obligation of the poet *as poet* toward his language is
restated as Aristotle had spoken of it, and Dante in defense
of the vulgar tongue; the reversal and re-reversal of beginning and end from *East Coker* are here, joined to the river
and sea, both specific and symbolic, of the poet's youth,
in the unceasing "exploration" of which the end "will be
to arrive where we started/ And know the place for the
first time." In the Quartets, "where we started" was the
rose-garden; and like the beginning the end will be through
the "unknown, remembered gate" into this garden, the old
hornèd gate into dreams that are true, not illusion. What
is true are those timeless moments in the garden, freed
from the enchainments of past and future, the chains of
the "crafty demon and the loud beast" of "hatred and
desire," moments in time but "free of time's covenant";
and in the garden are heard the voices of promise, "the
children in the apple-tree" with—if I am right about their
origin—their hint of the love and the Christ-child of the
fairy tale. Even now these moments are not the actual
mystical union with the Divine, but they are the final
assurance of its truth, with its promise that

> all shall be well . . .
> When the tongues of flame are in-folded
> Into the crowned knot of fire
> And the fire and the rose are one.

Superficially, the structure of the individual Quartets

seems not unlike that of *The Waste Land* or *The Hollow
Men*, a succession of contrasting and variegated blocks
differing in matter, mood, and style, *Burnt Norton* moving
from rose-garden to London Tube, from mystical still point
to the poet's difficulty in writing poems, from highly
wrought lyric verse almost to prose; and the others similarly. The coarse episodes of *The Waste Land* are absent,
and its miscellaneous figures—the Mrs. Equitones, Smyrna
merchants, and typists—are absent. Yet in terms of the
reader's intellectual grasp, the unified structure of *The
Waste Land* is clearer than that of any of the Quartets,
for in the earlier poem all the episodes function logically
as illustration and hence stand in an unequivocal contribu-
tory relation to one theme. This is not true of the Quartets,
where the structure is analogous rather to the thematic
pluralism of large musical forms, to which nothing in poetic
convention corresponds. Though in *Burnt Norton*, for
example, the religious and the mystical keep hovering in
the air, they do not explicitly, or even implicitly, control
the passages concerned with the poet's calling, its discour-
agements, and its technical difficulties: the connections
that might have been made are for the most part avoided.
There is compensation in the more homogeneous tone that
prevails through the variety in these late poems: they
contain no mockery, no satire, no parody, scarcely even
any wit; and, indeed, little of the external world is seen
otherwise than through reverie except for the particular
place which in each poem functions as a center from which
the meditations spring. The deeper center of each Quartet
separately and of all together, insofar as it can be formulat-
ed verbally, resides in their meditative projection of the
whole man (leaving aside specific social and personal
human relationships), Eliot as Christian and Eliot as poet.

In *Four Quartets* Eliot had undertaken a composite work
on the grand scale, not quite Dante's scale but obviously
with Dante in mind. Individually the poems contain pas-

sages that rank with his finest work: most of *Burnt Norton*,
I think, but especially the scene in the rose garden, the
"garlic and sapphires" lyric, and in its different way much
of the contrasting scene in the London Tube; scattered
passages in *East Coker* and *The Dry Salvages*; much of
Little Gidding, though one remembers most vividly several
lyric stanzas and the night scene of the "dead patrol";
many other fine short passages and memorable lines in
all four poems. Dante, however, had been wise enough to
let himself be shown his vision and be explained to; Eliot
tells us and shows us. The difference, superficially only
one of technical "point of view," in reality affects the
prevailing tone as well. Eliot, in short, does preach and
expound, sometimes in platitudes or in an almost coy
phrase that tempts the reader to mockery: no context can
absorb, in *East Coker*, "I shall say it again./ Shall I say
it again?" The tone that results, in many of the conversational, reflective, or hortatory passages, is unsure, for Eliot
underestimates his reader and at the same time has his
reader too much in mind. The arrogance of the younger
Eliot had been subdued by the Christian; but now in spite
of a sincere striving for humility, a complacent or conde-
scending tone is audible through certain of the more prosaic
passages and even in several of the lyrics.

In retrospect also I think one is apt to feel an absence
of vitality and a thinness of substance, occasions when
Eliot seems to be filling out a form too large for what
he had to say, or for the energy at his disposal. He had
chosen for his poems a most difficult form, for he gave
himself no support from narrative, which might have been
to a degree self-propelling; nor was he writing a systematic
philosophical poem or series of poems in which an intellectual structure might conceivably have provided energy and
form of another sort. He created his own structure for
the individual quartet with no closer prototype than the
analogue of a musical form. This gave freshness and

inspired some fine effects: but it made demands to which he could not always rise.

It is too early for a final judgment on the *Four Quartets* as a whole. They are now only some thirty-odd years old, and that is not long enough to test the durability of any but certain of the finest passages. As these are not easily extractable and so cannot be anthologized without loss, one must hope that, uneven as they are, the Quartets will survive whole, imperfections and all. *Burnt Norton*, at least, and most of *Little Gidding*, seem to me to have this durability.

11

The Self-Contained

Continuity and change together are inclusive enough to sum up everybody's life and are therefore meaningless except when particular continuities and changes are traced in a particular life-and-work or in the rare instance when they become the watchful, conscious preoccupation of the individual who undertakes to shape into a particular pattern his own continuities and changes, and to parallel this in another created pattern of objective correlatives. Though I have said "rare," I can in fact think of no English poet other than Eliot who seems deliberately to have shaped his poetic life in these terms.

The whole of Shakespeare's plays and poems may well present, as Eliot said, a single developing personality, may even be felt as "one poem." But though we no longer mistake Shakespeare for the child of nature he was once thought to be, we do not, either, see in his work the deliberate *construction* of an objectified, consistent personality. There was some such impulse in Wordsworth, who worked directly upon his own experience in building the cathedral with its side-chapels that he never completed.

But even in *The Prelude*, or elsewhere when he could say
the child is father of the man or could describe the effect
upon himself of the French Revolution and a love affair,
Wordsworth did not really watch himself developing and
did not expressly create a poetic self of development and
continuity; he had not that kind of self-consciousness. Nor
is it what we find in Yeats, for all his autobiographical
immediacies, his self-consciousness so different from Eliot's,
his extraordinary development, and the essential unity of
his work: Yeats still had his many identities, all of them
real and all of them mask, as Yeats very well knew. Still
less do we find it in any minor poets that I can think
of. The whole of Eliot's poetry, and the plays as well insofar
as they contribute to the significant whole, deliberately
present a unified and "developing personality"—a personality of a unique kind too for a poet, since it springs from
the sort of temperament that is scarcely ever free enough
to be creative. We started with *Prufrock*, and we have to
ask where we end: is it, in sum, with Prufrock still?

Prufrock was solitary, knew that he was, accepted essential character as fate, and looked forward in resignation
to an unchanging life. The rather more vital man behind
Prufrock, instead, ventured out into the world of human
beings, of sex, of external insecurity; found it bitter; said
so by projections of disgust bordering on horrors, getting
back at the human race through the Burbanks and Bleis-
teins and pimpled adolescents, taking refuge in the exercise
of technical skill and ingenuities of mosaic constructions;
found refuge and a function for himself in concern with
theories of "tradition" and "unity of culture," and satisfaction in the role (even in youth) of society's elder critic;
found the darkened spirit could still create by looking
outward upon a waste land of moral and emotional distortions, a world of the heartless and the irresponsible, which
might—just might—be saved by the cultivation of human
decency ("give, sympathize, control"). But this proves after

all no solution, cannot be believed to work for the world
or unreservedly practiced. A renewed Christianity becomes
the one hope: for the world at large a discipline and perhaps
a way of devotion; for the solitary self these, and also a
human relationship, acceptable perhaps because less individual than institutional, relieving solitude without invad-
ing it. It is a relationship costing, the poet says, "not less
than everything"; but that full price only the saint and
the mystic need pay, for the rest of us to a degree control
our paying and giving. Even such a conversion for such
a temperament is not easy; but ultimately intellect and
will and feeling reach a certain harmony—if not perfect,
at least a degree of harmony—that leaves no utterly
unreconciled dominant seventh crying out for resolution,
and one that does, at its least, include a great deal more
of the world than Prufrock's stasis could accommodate.

The poetry remains solitary. Throughout that most
populous of poems, *The Waste Land,* no voice ever answers
another voice aloud. Eliot was not a love poet except for
one late, intimate poem addressed to his second wife; or
a poet of friendship beyond one occasional poem written
for Walter de la Mare and brief, jaunty lines to Ralph
Hodgson. Otherwise what is striking is the all but complete
absence of human relationship. Of felt relationships there
are a few ambiguous glimpses only, and even significant
chance encounters are rare: no leech gatherer or Margaret
or Ruth stirred him to reflective poetry. When the poems
turn to religion, love is spoken of but not expressed. Unlike
a Herbert or a Hopkins, who loved God and loved Christ
personally and intimately (the skeptic may think
anthropomorphically), Eliot—the Eliot of the poems—
strives for belief, for a Christian way of life, strives to
remould thought, feeling, speech into those of the Church,
but conceives Christian Love in abstract impersonal terms.
Love is honored as the center of the last lyric in *Little
Gidding,* but as a doubly symbolic abstraction, descending

as both the bomber of wartime and the Holy Spirit:

Who then devised the torment? Love.
Love is the unfamiliar Name
Behind the hands that wove
The intolerable shirt of flame
Which human power cannot remove.

Whether a radical change of personality ever occurs
may be uncertain; that of the developing personality
recorded in Eliot's poetry, at any rate, is not so radical
as to compel doubt of either its poetic or its personal reality.
The other, perhaps partly compensatory, side of that poetic
personality, the arrogance not apparent in the person
Prufrock but evident enough in the poem that gives him
to us, enters the poetry by fits and starts till it is officially
subdued; after that, unofficially it becomes a serious defect
in *The Rock* and is modified only into an over-readiness
for the oracular in parts of the *Quartets*. Even the aridity
of the early work, consciously "distinguished aridity" there,
reappears unacknowledged from time to time; and now,
being unacknowledged and hence not made use of, becomes
occasionally a blemish and finally more than a blemish,
a mark of failure of creation, in the plays. On the other
hand, in the poetry beginning with *Ash Wednesday*, there
is compensation in a much greater poetic freedom.

A summary is a simplification, and a summary of a
lifetime's poetic achievement a gross simplification. But
it is one way of trying to make more precisely visible to
oneself what G. M. Hopkins would have called the "inscape" of the work—indeed, the double inscape: that of
the whole unique *oeuvre* and that of the individually
unique poem; the hallmark of the poetry as a whole which
is part of the essence of each; that which makes a Matisse
a Matisse as well as a fine painting, that which bends a
painter's technique into a "characteristic" work. There is

an irresistible interest in trying to make out, however inadequately, the pattern that one such artist creates in a poetic history that begins, say, with a cocky "Cousin Harriet, here is the Boston Evening Transcript," and ends with Pentecostal tongues of flame.

Note on Texts and
References

Except where otherwise indicated, quotations from the poems follow the text of *Collected Poems* 1909-1962 (New York: Harcourt, Brace and World, 1963), supplemented by *Four Quartets* (New York: Harcourt, Brace, 1943); *Poems Written in Early Youth* (New York: Farrar, Straus and Giroux, 1967); *The Waste Land: A Facsimile and Transcript of the Original Drafts Including the Annotations of Ezra Pound*, ed. Valerie Eliot (London: Faber and Faber, 1971; abbreviated in the notes as *WL Facs.*) Of the plays, *Murder in the Cathedral* is cited from the New York edition of Harcourt, Brace, 1935; *The Family Reunion* from that of Harcourt, 1939; *The Confidential Clerk* from London: Faber and Faber, 1954.

The following editions of Eliot's prose have been frequently cited:

Selected Essays. London: Faber and Faber, 1951 (reprinted 1953). Abbreviated in notes as *SE*.

On Poetry and Poets. New York: Farrar, Straus and Cudahy, 1957. Abbreviated as *P and P*.

To Criticize the Critic. New York: Farrar, Straus and Giroux, 1965. Abbreviated as *CC*.

The Use of Poetry and the Use of Criticism. Cambridge (Mass.): Harvard University Press, 1933.
After Strange Gods. London: Faber and Faber, 1934.

I have also made occasional use of the second edition of *The Sacred Wood* (Knopf reprint, New York: 1930).

The following works by others are frequently cited. They are identified in the notes by the author's or editor's last name:

Donald Gallup. *T. S. Eliot: A Bibliography* (rev. and extended ed.). New York: Harcourt, Brace and World, 1969.

Helen Gardner. *The Art of T. S. Eliot.* New York: Dutton, 1950.

Herbert Howarth. *Notes on Some Figures behind T. S. Eliot.* London: Chatto and Windus, 1967.

Hugh Kenner. *The Invisible Poet: T. S. Eliot.* New York: McDowell, Obolensky, 1959.

A. Walton Litz, ed. *Eliot in His Time.* Princeton: Princeton University Press, 1973.

Richard March and Tambimuttu, eds.. *T. S. Eliot.* Chicago: Henry Regnery, 1949.

F. O. Matthiessen. *The Achievement of T. S. Eliot* (rev. and enlarged ed.). New York: Oxford University Press, 1947.

B. Rajan, ed. *T. S. Eliot: A Study of His Writings by Several Hands.* New York: Funk and Wagnalls, 1948.

Grover Smith. *T. S. Eliot's Poetry and Plays.* Chicago: University of Chicago Press, 1956.

Allen Tate, ed. *T. S. Eliot: The Man and His Work.* London: Chatto and Windus, 1967.

Writers at Work: The Paris Review Interviews. Second series. New York: Viking, 1965. Abbreviated in notes as *Paris Interviews.*

Notes

Chapter 1: Introduction

[1] The successive statements on personality occur in "Tradition and the Individual Talent" (1919), "Shakespeare and the Stoicism of Seneca" (1927), "Dante" (1929), all in *SE*, pp. 17-21, 137, 273; and "The Three Voices of Poetry" (1953), *P and P*, pp. 103-104; those on personality and the whole *oeuvre* appear in Eliot's introduction to G. Wilson Knight's *The Wheel of Fire* (London: Methuen, 1965, reprinted from the edition of 1930), p. xvii; "John Ford" (1932), *SE*, pp. 193-194, 203 (and cf. a similar brief statement in the essay on Dante about the "pattern in Shakespeare's carpet" in comparison with Dante's "pattern," p. 245); "Hamlet" (1919), *SE*, p. 146.

[2] "The Frontiers of Criticism" (1956), *P and P*, p. 117 (and cf. "The Music of Poetry," p. 17).

Chapter 2: The Search for a Style

[1] "Yeats," in *P and P*, p. 295. Elsewhere Eliot acknowledged his great debt to Symons for this introduction. For more detailed accounts of Symbolist influence, see René Taupin, *L'Influence du symbolisme français sur la poésie américaine de 1910 à 1920* (Paris: Champion, 1929) and Edmund Wilson, *Axel's Castle* (New York: Scribner, 1931), as well as the third chapter of D. E. S. Maxwell's *The Poetry of T. S. Eliot* (London: Routledge and Kegan Paul, 1952).

[2] *John Davidson: A Selection of His Poems*, with a preface by T. S. Eliot, ed. with an introduction by Maurice Lindsay (London: Hutchinson, 1961). My quotations are from the unpaged preface of Eliot and from

Lindsay's introduction, pp. 8-9, quoting from Eliot's recorded broadcast.

³ *SE*, p. 237, and *Paris Interviews*, pp. 98-99.

⁴ "What Dante Means to Me," *CC*, p. 126.

⁵ Identified in Smith, p. 28.

Chapter 3: *Prufrock*

¹ March and Tambimuttu, p. 20.

² *WL Facs.* p. ix.

³ *Ibid.*, p. xxii (6 November, 1921).

Chapter 4: The Widening Gyre

¹ *Paris Interviews*, p. 97.

² *WL Facs.*, p. xviii.

³ Matthiessen, p. 129, is the earliest source I know for this statement (apparently made in conversation) though it has been repeated by many writers. The actual words appear to be Matthiessen's.

⁴ Eliot's review of *Quia Pauper Amavi* (reprinting *Homage to Sextus Propertius*), "The Method of Mr. Pound," in the *Athenaeum* for 24 October, 1919. The passage is also quoted in Howarth, p. 132.

⁵ Kenner, p. 112.

⁶ See ch. 28, "The Height of Knowledge"; ch. 6, "Rome (1859-1860)"; ch. 33, "A Dynamic Theory of History."

⁷ Quoted in "Reflections on 'Vers Libre'" and "Ezra Pound: His Metric and Poetry," reprinted in *CC*, pp. 180 and 186. Eliot might also, however, have been remembering the "multiplying mirrors" of Yeats's essay "The Symbolism of Poetry" in *Ideas of Good and Evil*.

⁸ Correspondence in *TLS*, 11 May, 1973.

⁹ *CC*, p. 16 (written in 1961). Cf. the similar statement of 1942 in "The Music of Poetry" (*P and P*, p. 17) and the statement, quoted here once before, that the best of his criticism had been "a by-product of [his] private poetry-workshop."

¹⁰ *SE*, pp. 18-21.

Chapter 5: *The Waste Land*

¹ "T. S. Eliot: Some Literary Impressions," in Tate, pp. 253-254.

² "In Memory of Henry James," *Egoist* V (January 1916), 1-2.

³ Review of *Ulysses* in the *Dial*, November 1923. *Ulysses* was published in book form in the same year as *The Waste Land*, but Eliot knew and admired it earlier. See the account in Howarth, pp. 242-245.

⁴ *WL Facs.*, p. xxii.

⁵ *TLS*, 20 September, 1923, under the title "A Fragmentary Poem"; Lucas in *New Statesman and Nation*, 3 November, 1923. In spite of reviews, the poem sold rather better than had been expected.

⁶ "Thoughts after Lambeth" (1931), *SE*, p. 368; *WL Facs.*, p. [1].

⁷ *SE*, p. 405; *WL Facs.*, p. 129.

[8] Letter of 15 October, 1923, Bertrand Russell, *Autobiography*, 3 vols. (London: Allen and Unwin, 1967-1969), II:173.

[9] *WL Facs.*, p. x; Pound, *Letters*, ed. D. D. Paige (New York: Harcourt, 1950), p. 180; *CC*, p. 34.

[10] *Paris Interviews*, p. 100.

[11] *WL Facs.*, pp. x, xviii, xxi. For further discussion of the probable dates of composition, see the essays by Ellmann, Gardner, and Kenner in the Litz volume, and the detailed analysis of available evidence by Grover Smith in "The Making of *The Waste Land*," *Mosaic* VI/1 (Fall 1972), pp. 128-41. Briefly, "The Fire Sermon," or that part of it which precedes the "Thames Daughters" passage, is thought to have been written by the summer or even spring of 1921, before Eliot left London in October; most of the rest later that year, partly perhaps at Margate, mainly at Lausanne. At that time, passages written earlier may have been incorporated, especially in Parts I and IV. This is a rough summary of complicated and uncertain evidence, but it suffices for the purpose of my discussion. None of the passages suspected of being the earliest includes material dependent on Jessie Weston's book.

[12] Eliot's introduction to Pound's *Selected Poems* (1928), quoted also in *WL Facs.*, p. 127.

[13] Since this was written, the Litz volume has been published, and Professor Litz himself makes significant observations on the non-narrative method of the poem (pp. 5-7). See also his discussion of the history and significance of Eliot's notes to the poem, pp. 9-16.

[14] *Life for Life's Sake* (New York: Viking, 1941), p. 272. Aldington says he has confirmed his memory through official weather reports for that year.

Chapter 6: *Hollow Men* and *Sweeney*

[1] *Nation and Athenaeum* XXXIV, 6 October, 1923, pp. 11-12.

[2] *Journal* (New York: Viking, 1933), pp. 786-787. The conversation was a continuation of that referred to earlier concerning *The Waste Land*. The plan was carried out and Bennett saw the samples.

[3] *SE*, pp. 111-113; *Sacred Wood*, p. 70.

[4] Conclusion to *The Use of Poetry*, pp. 146-147. For analysis of *Sweeney* in terms of more recent drama, see William V. Spanos, " 'Wanna Go Home, Baby?': *Sweeney Agonistes* as Drama of the Absurd," *PMLA*, LXXXV (January 1970), 8-20.

[5] For earlier discussions of *The Hollow Men*, see especially those of Smith, pp. 99-109, to which I am indebted, and Kenner, pp. 183-194, who has interesting comments on, among other things, the style and the epigraphs. George Williamson, in *A Reader's Guide to T. S. Eliot* (New York: Noonday, 1953), pp. 154-162, had in some points anticipated them, as all three, and others, have anticipated me. For a discussion of Dowson as a possible source for the title and one line of the poem, see Geoffrey Tillotson, *Essays in Criticism and Research*, (Hamden, Conn.: Archon, 1967), pp. 153-156 (the essay includes Eliot's comments).

The origin of the two epigraphs is common knowledge: "Mistah Kurtz—he dead" from Conrad's *Heart of Darkness* (a longer passage on the death of Kurtz had originally introduced *The Waste Land*) and "A penny for the Old Guy," referring to Guy Fawkes Day (the effigy of Guy Fawkes and the children begging pennies for fireworks).

[6] *The Use of Poetry*, p. 144.

[7] "John Dryden," *SE*, pp. 314-315.

[8] This line closed the lyric when it was published in *Criterion*; though absent from the final poem, it seems clearly enough implied.

[9] *The Use of Poetry*, p. 148.

Chapter 7: *Ash Wednesday*

[1] From a talk on "Christianity and Communism" in *The Listener*, quoted by D. Margolis in *T. S. Eliot's Intellectual Development 1922-1939* (Chicago: University of Chicago Press, 1972), p. 106. Margolis provides the best and fullest account now available of Eliot's conversion. An earlier, more personal account by Robert Sencourt in *T. S. Eliot: A Memoir* (ed. Donald Adamson), chapter 10, clearly stands in need of confirmation and correction from other sources. The discussion in Kristian Smidt (*Poetry and Belief in the Work of T. S. Eliot* 1949, 1961) is rather topical than chronological.

[2] *SE*, pp. 483-484, 491; the essays on Babbitt and Bradley are also reprinted in this volume. In a recent detailed article, "Eliot and Hulme in 1916: Toward a Revaluation of Eliot's Critical and Spiritual Development," Ronald Schuchard argues for an early as well as sustained influence upon Eliot of Hulme's thought (*PMLA* LXXXVIII [October 1973], 1083-1094).

[3] "The Literature of Fascism," *Criterion* VIII (December 1928), 283.

[4] Cf. John 1:1-14; and Andrewes's Nativity sermon of 1611, "What, *Verbum infans*, the Word of an infant? The Word, and not be able to speak a word?" Eliot quoted the passage in *SE*, p. 350.

[5] *SE*, pp. 243, 262-263.

Chapter 8: The Ariel Poems and *Coriolan*

[1] *Purgatorio*, Canto XVI: 85-96, the Okey translation, which is the one Eliot had used when he quoted the passage earlier in his essay on Sir John Davies. I have changed the order of words at the beginning, so as to open with the verb as Dante does and as Eliot does in the poem.

[2] *SE*, p. 350.

[3] P. 141.

[4] Quoted by Elizabeth Drew in *T. S. Eliot: The Design of His Poetry* (New York: Scribner, 1949), p. 127.

[5] The statement was made in the postscript of a letter (9 May 1930) to Sir Michael Sadler enclosing the MS and typescripts of the poem. My information is from the Houghton Library's photostat of the original, now in the Bodleian.

[6] Knight, "T. S. Eliot: Some Literary Impressions" in Tate, pp. 247-249.
[7] *SE*, p. 144.
[8] Smith, p. 159, quoting from a Chicago Round Table series.
[9] *Criterion* VIII, 288.

Chapter 9: Pattern in the Carpet

[1] *SE*, pp. 137, 126, and *passim*.
[2] *SE*, p. 245 (see also pp. 184, 189); and Eliot's introduction to Wilson Knight's *Wheel of Fire*.
[3] *WL Facs.*, pp. [118]-[121] and note.
[4] Eliot's chief use of Andrewes came somewhat later, but he had begun to read him in 1921 or before. See Howarth, p. 222 and note to that page, p. 375.
[5] Gardner, p. 159.
[6] *Ushant*, p. 179.
[7] *After Strange Gods*, pp. 16, 55.
[8] For a full and more sympathetic treatment of the plays, see David E. Jones, *The Plays of T. S. Eliot* (London: Routledge and Kegan Paul, 1960).

Chapter 10: *Four Quartets*

[1] *P and P*, p. 98.
[2] Quoted by Matthiessen, p. 90, from an unpublished lecture delivered in New Haven in 1933. Eliot said he had long aimed at this ideal, but his formulation of it is obviously prospective, not retrospective.
[3] Reprinted New York: Knopf, 1944. For Beethoven and Sullivan (whom Eliot knew personally) see Howarth, pp. 277-289, and his article "Eliot, Beethoven, and J. W. N. Sullivan," *Comparative Lit.* IX (1957), 322-332; for Bartók, see the testimony of M. J. C. Hodgart cited in Kenner, p. 306. Howarth draws attention to some of the points and a few of the passages in Sullivan to which I refer.
[4] "The Music of Poetry," (1942), *P and P*, p. 32.
[5] Sullivan, pp. 229-231, 239-241.
[6] London: Macmillan, 1918, pp. 85-87.
[7] This is in the third movement of the A minor quartet. Sullivan quotes the main part of Beethoven's superscriptions and describes the movement at considerable length (pp. 243-246).
[8] Sullivan, p. 256.
[9] Preface to Eliot's translation of St. J. Perse's *Anabasis*.
[10] The millionaire was identified as Adam by Eliot himself, according to Raymond Preston in *Four Quartets Rehearsed* (London: Sheed, Ward, 1948), p. 34.
[11] For fuller and generally far more favorable discussions of *East Coker*, see Smith, pp. 268-277; Gardner, pp. 38-76 *passim* and 164-170; James John Sweeny (1941) as reprinted in Bergonzi's *Casebook*, pp. 36-56.

[12] *After Strange Gods,* p. 29.

[13] "T. S. Eliot's *Quartets: A New Reading,*" reprinted from *Studies* (1965) in Bergonzi's *Casebook,* pp. 212-236; for this movement, see p. 230.

[14] Bhagavad-Gita II (tr. Probhavananda and Isherwood).

Index

Page references to essays of Eliot quoted in the text, but identified by title only in the notes, are printed in brackets.